CORNWALL

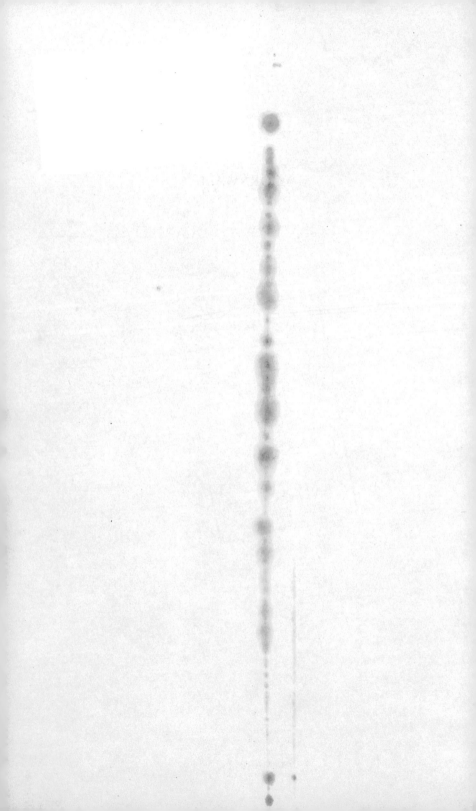

Robin Davidson

CORNWALL

B. T. Batsford Ltd
London

Acknowledgements

The Author and Publishers would like to thank the following for permission to reproduce the photographs in this book: Peter Baker Photography Ltd, nos 11, 13, 21, 24; G. Douglas Bolton, no. 3; the late Noel Habgood, nos 5, 22; Richard Hawken, nos 2, 4, 6, 10; A. F. Kersting, nos 1, 7, 8, 9, 12, 14–20, 23, 25. The map is by Patrick Leeson.

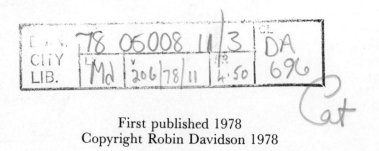

First published 1978
Copyright Robin Davidson 1978

Phototypeset by Trident Graphics Ltd,
Reigate, Surrey

Printed in Great Britain by
J. W. Arrowsmith Ltd, Bristol
for the publishers B. T. Batsford Ltd
4 Fitzhardinge Street, London W1H 0AH
ISBN 0 7134 0588 0

Contents

		page
	Acknowledgements	
	List of Illustrations	
	Map of Cornwall	
	Introduction: The Landscapes of Cornwall	7
1	Launceston and the South-East	16
2	The North-East and Bodmin Moor	32
3	The Southern Moor and the Looe Rivers	49
4	Fowey and St Austell	61
5	North Mid-Cornwall	78
6	Around the Fal	109
7	Industrial Revolution Country	125
8	The Southern Peninsula	144
9	The Far West	158
	A Guide to Cornish Place-Names	171
	Sites to Visit	172
	Index	174

Illustrations

1 Lanhydrock House 81
2 Trerice Manor 81
3 Morwenstow church 82
4 The Cheesewring 83
5 Polperro 84
6 Mending nets, Mevagissey 84
7 A china clay pit near St Austell 85
8 Restormel Castle 86
9 Rough Tor 86
10 Respryn Bridge 87
11 Wadebridge 87
12 Truro Cathedral 88
13 The harbour, St Ives 89
14 The harbour, Falmouth 89
15 Medieval cross, Lostwithiel churchyard 90
16 Monument in Mevagissey church 90
17 Base of the rood screen, St Levan church 90
18 Crackington Haven 91
19 Abandoned engine-house, Rinsey Head 91
20 St Austell church 92
21 Gunwalloe church 92
22 St Michael's Mount 93
23 The Market House, Penzance 94
24 Sennen Cove 95
25 Land's End and the Longships Lighthouse 96

Introduction

Six miles south of Hartland Point, where the majestic cliffs are buffeted by the Atlantic gales, a lonely stream hurries down a steep and wooded valley to the sea at Marsland Mouth. Cross this stream and you leave Devon behind you; and not only Devon but—in the opinion of many—England. Cornishmen are very conscious that their county boundary is a frontier, and certainly no county has so clearly defined a line of demarcation. For within a few hundred yards of the source of this little stream rises another, the Tamar, which turns south and flows almost 60 miles to the English Channel. And for virtually all its length, this river acts as the boundary, the frontier of a land set apart from the rest of the country, possessing its own language and inheriting a tradition very much its own. Separated by stream and river from the rest of England, and confronting the sea for 200 miles on its other sides, Cornwall is a world of its own.

But within this world there is a wealth of contrast. There is really no such thing as a typical Cornish landscape, since the county offers such diversity. To begin with, its coastline—and that is what Cornwall means to most people—has great variety. The county is rather like a giant slice of cake, sloping to the south: the north coast defies the sea in a series of magnificent cliffs, backed by a high plateau of good agricultural land. The watershed, or spine of the county, lies to the north, and a series of river valleys run to the south coast. Here the tide flows many miles up the estuaries, up the drowned river valleys of the Tamar and the Fowey, the Fal and the Helford. Many smaller streams flow from the inland moors into the larger rivers or to the sea, but few make for the north coast: the Camel is the only major river system on this side of the county.

And what of the inland landscape? Here too is variety, with the river valleys of east Cornwall, the industrial scene of the mining districts and the china clay areas, and the wild moorland. Each area has its own character, its own interest and its individual beauty, and to neglect inland Cornwall in quest of the coast is a mistake.

The history of the formation of the landscape carries us back through millions of years, a story of convulsions of the earth and the gradual building up of sedimentary rocks. For uncounted centuries wind, sun and

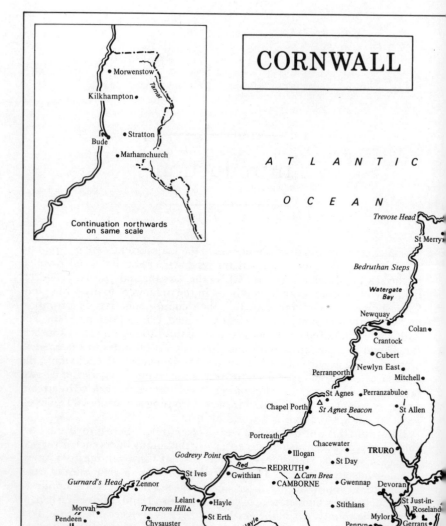

DEVON

Crackington Haven

Boscastle

Tintagel • Bossinney
Camel
Camelford

LAUNCESTON
Inny
Polston Bridge

Altarnun
Greyston Bridge

Port Isaac   Rough Tor △ △ Brown Willy   Lewannick
St Endellion   B O D M Y N
St Breward   North Hill
St Minver   • St Tudy   M O O R   Bolventor
Padstock   Horse Bridge
Little   Wadebridge   • Blisland   Dozmary Pool   Linkinhorne   Gunnislake
Petherick   St Breock   Egloshayle   New Bridge
                        • Helland   Warleggan   Callington
                     Cardinham •   • St Cleer
              • BODMIN   Fowey •   St Neot
St Wenn   Liskeard •   • Menheniot
St Columb Major   West Loose   Landrake
            • Roche   East Loose   St Germans   Saltash
        Lanlivery • • Lostwithiel   Seaton
St Dennis   • Luxulyan   Lerryn   • Lanreath   Torpoint
        St Blazey • Golant • Pelynt •
adock   Par • • Tywardreath   Lansallos   Looe   Whitesand   Cawsand
    ST AUSTELL • Charlestown Fowey • • Talland   Bay   Bay
      Porthpean •   Polperro
Probus   Pentewan   Gribbin Head   Rame Head
regony   St Ewe •
        St Michael • Mevagissey
        Caerhays • Gorran   Bodrugan's Leap
Veryan   • Gorran Haven
      Portloe   Dodman Point
Nare Head

E N G L I S H   C H A N N E L

0   5   10 miles

water changed the shape and composition of the land. Cataclysmic upheavals forced molten material through the layers of slate and sandstone to form areas of granite and create veins of metal, all of which were to play such an important part in Cornwall's history. During the aeons of time while life was evolving, the sea advanced and receded, until the final retreat of the ice determined the existing shape of the land, the Cornwall we see now.

Four principal areas of granite occur in the county, Bodmin Moor in the east, Hensbarrow Downs north of St Austell, Carnmenellis south of Redruth, and the far west peninsula of Penwith. The effects of weathering over the centuries have produced curious rock formations like the Cheesewring on Bodmin Moor and 'logan rocks' or rocking stones. It is small wonder that primitive men saw the hands of giants in these stones and peopled the land with spirits: the moors have a sombre atmosphere and a presence that is often uncomfortable.

Primitive men have themselves left visible evidence of their presence throughout the county. Only Wiltshire can rival the prehistoric remains which stand as witness to the early inhabitants. Of the Old and Middle Stone Ages little can be seen, apart from some coastal sites which were probably only temporary settlements. But with the arrival of Neolithic Man, approximately 5,000 years ago, we have the evidence of permanent occupation, for these people were farmers and developed the land where they settled. Several flint factories existed, providing a source of trade, and the remains of Neolithic occupation have been found on Carn Brea near Camborne.

The durability of the stone has resulted in the widespread survival of megalithic tombs and stone circles, which largely date from the second millenium B.C. The stone circles are to be found either in the eastern part of the county or in the far west. Legend relates that the several groups of Nine Maidens were petrified for profaning the sabbath by dancing and that the Hurlers suffered the same fate for similarly ill-timed indulgence in the good Cornish sport of hurling. If medieval moralists saw fit to preach such sermons in stones, we can at least be grateful for the attractive names and think what we like as we gaze at the Pipers or the Merry Maidens.

During the Bronze Age period, trade developed in western Europe. Cornwall lay directly across the trading route between western Britain and Ireland to the north and France and the Mediterranean to the south. Rather than risk the hazards of rounding Land's End, merchants preferred to land their cargo in Cornwall and use an overland route to the opposite coast. Two routes were chiefly used: one across the narrow neck of land between St Ives Bay and Mount's Bay by way of the Hayle River, and the other from the Camel estuary to the Fowey. So we can imagine the small boats moored in the estuaries, the loading and unloading of their cargoes and the strings of pack animals threading their way over the ancient inland tracks.

The pattern of life in Cornwall was little changed for centuries until the arrival of Celtic immigrants, who gave renewed impetus to agriculture. The principal evidence of Iron Age settlement now lies in hill-top fortifications. But since a main source of attack lay from the sea, so there developed a series of cliff castles on promontories such as Trevelgue Head and Kelsey Head near Newquay, or Black Head and the Dodman on the south coast. Traces of several Iron Age villages of courtyard houses have come to light, mostly in the Penwith area, the most remarkable being the village of Chysauster in the parish of Gulval. Here and at some other villages such as Carn Euny and Porthmeor we can also see subterranean galleries roofed in stone known as fogous, another witness to human life and occupation before the Christian era.

By this time Britain had come within the sway of the Roman Empire. This western extremity had little attraction for the Romans in mineral resources—tin was obtainable more accessibly in Spain—and the inhabitants were not hostile enough to warrant full-scale military occupation. With the departure of the Romans the mists of the Dark Ages settle over the history of Cornwall, the stories of Arthur and King Mark and the lives of the Celtic saints whose names are commemorated all over the county contributing to the mixture of fact and legend. Eventually the Saxons conquered Cornwall, and they in their turn gave place to the Normans. Perhaps the most characteristic reminders of this period are the stone crosses which occur all over Cornwall.

The Normans imposed the firm hand of their authority in Cornwall as in the rest of the country with forbidding castles. Though nothing on the grand scale is now to be seen, the best preserved remains are at Trematon with its incomparable views over the Lynher and the Tamar, and Restormel perched high above the Fowey just north of Lostwithiel. What remains of Dunheved Castle at Launceston shows what a commanding position it held, and for an awe-inspiring situation little can rival the headland castle at Tintagel.

Another aspect of the activity of the Normans was the spur to church building which they provided. The characteristics of the typical Cornish church are homeliness and simplicity rather than grandeur or elaboration. To talk of a typical church is actually as meaningless as a typical landscape, since there is so much variety in detail, but in general the pattern is of a fairly low nave, chancel and aisle, and a western tower. Many churches have Norman work, with numerous fonts surviving, but rebuilding and enlargement over the years often meant that the bulk of the original Norman work was superseded. Generally speaking, most Cornish churches are now fifteenth-century buildings, with various features of earlier or later dates. Spires are rare, and towers are low, displaying strength rather than grace, though there are several high-soaring examples.

By comparison Cornwall has not a great deal of post-Reformation church building to show, apart from a few Georgian churches and Truro cathedral, which is in a class of its own—and we must not overlook the abundance of nonconformist chapels, large and small, throughout the county. On the other hand, there is a wealth of domestic architecture, and perhaps the most notable feature of the Cornish scene is neither religious nor domestic, but industrial. The derelict engine-houses are a poignant reminder of the former greatness of mining. This reached its apogee in the eighteenth and nineteenth centuries, but with the closure of mines there was widespread emigration, and 'knackt bals' stand as melancholy memorials from Hingston Down in the east to the spectacular Botallack on the cliffs near Cape Cornwall.

The primary building material in Cornwall is stone, though the natural material for farm buildings and cottages was cob—a remarkably durable mixture of clay and chopped straw, capable of lasting for centuries, given a good dry foundation of stone and adequate roofing protection. Brick is rare and mostly found in the south-east; Cornwall has never had an abundance of timber for building. As a result stone is the basic material, which largely means slate and granite, though only comparatively recently have builders had the means of working granite with any ease; moor granite was used for centuries in preference to quarried granite. Slate stone came into its own as a roofing material, and the technique of slate-hanging for walls became quite widely employed.

Not only in buildings is stone very much in evidence but also in the hedges flanking the Cornish roads. These hedges usually take the form of massive ramparts, which vary in form according to the nature of the local stone. A characteristic construction is an earth bank faced with slate, often supporting a crown of bushes and small trees. If granite is accessible, however, the granite dry wall may be employed, with smaller stones set on top of larger foundation boulders and an earth mixture in the interstices. As a result the traveller along Cornish roads is frequently frustrated when his view of the countryside is blocked by a solid hedge, and tantalizing glimpses of scenery are visible at gateways. On the other hand the hedges are often filled with a variety of plant life, ferns in profusion and in some valleys the butter-yellow primroses gathered in rich clusters like cream.

With the opening up of communications, and especially the growth of the railway network, building materials could be brought from much further afield. For centuries, however, transport was difficult in Cornwall. In very early times the easiest form of communication was often by sea, and barges plied on the rivers. A few canals were constructed, but the landscape of Cornwall generally is not suitable for this purpose and little trace now remains of these ventures.

Most of the smaller roads grew up in a haphazard fashion as need arose, but the main roads in Cornwall followed the ridgeways of the higher ground, avoiding the marshy land of the valleys. So the oldest main route entered Cornwall well to the north, skirted the north of Bodmin Moor and kept to the spine of the county. Bridges were gradually built in medieval times as the need grew, but in many instances ferries are much older than bridges. The process of road construction was accelerated by the turnpike system, and many picturesque valley routes came into being. The coming of the motor car has altered the picture yet again. The pattern of roads was already in existence, but constant improvements have been necessitated: now the construction of dual-carriageway roads by-passing the towns is the only way to try to deal with the vast influx of traffic pouring into Cornwall in the summer months.

Years before the time of the motor car, however, the railways had arrived. Individual railway links were established in various parts of Cornwall during the first half of the nineteenth century, many of these originally for industrial purposes. The nature of the terrain called for great skill in railway construction; trains often emerge from cuttings bright with valerian and rhododendron to cross deep valleys on soaring viaducts. The engineer responsible for much of the work was Brunel, and it was in 1859 that his masterpiece was completed—the Saltash Bridge.

This achievement was decisive. Cornwall's semi-isolated status was lost: London was only hours away. The traditional industries were dying, but the tourist traffic was now to flow in to take their place, receiving renewed impetus with the development of motor transport. It is difficult for the modern visitor—or the modern resident—to picture Cornwall before the opening up of communications, but any view of history that does not consider this aspect is bound to be distorted.

So much for the communication between the centres of population: what now of the centres themselves? Cornwall possesses no large cities, and is on the whole a land of small communities. Some larger settlements arose as ecclesiastical or market centres, such as Bodmin, Launceston and Truro. Around the coast fishing villages developed, and with the industrial boom of the eighteenth and nineteenth centuries towns such as Redruth, Camborne and St Austell grew rapidly. Finally the growth of tourism led to the expansion, or transformation, of places such as Penzance, Newquay and St Ives. But the little hamlet remains a typical feature of the Cornish landscape, and the county is predominantly rural in character.

One feature of Cornish settlements which the local people accept without a second thought but which immediately impresses the visitor is their names. What music they contain: Luxulyan, Mevagissey, Goonhavern, Praze-an-Beeble, Porthgwarra—how un-English they sound. And un-English they are. The ancient linguistic separation of the Cornish and the English is nowhere more clear than in the names.

> By *Tre, Ros, Car, Lan, Pol* and *Pen*
> You well may known all Cornishmen

runs the old saying, and the visitor makes a start if he knows that *tre* means a homestead, *pol* a pool and *pen* a head or headland, that *lan* indicates a sacred settlement, *car* a camp and *ros* a heath.

The interpretation of Cornish names is a fascinating study and they are among the glories of the county. One could not invent more attractive names, and they are a precious part of our heritage: Tolgroggan, Halabezack, Hendravossan—one could go on indefinitely. And again, the army of saints' names cannot go unnoticed. Some sound straightforward enough, like St Anthony, or St Clement, but who was St Veep? Or St Tudy or St Erney? The Cornish signposts point not only to places, but back through the centuries, to a past where fact and legend become intertwined, so that even the signposts have their fascination.

Cornwall is a world of its own but also a region of contrast and variety. Many people—visitors and residents alike—claim to know the 'real' Cornwall, and are prepared to defend their particular area against all other claims. Yet who is prepared to arbitrate in such a debate? Part of the charm of the county lies in its infinite variety. By way of preparation for our closer examination of the landscape, let us follow the steps of the giants of Cornwall's mythical past, striding from one hill to the next.

Come first to Kit Hill in the south-east, where the wind blows round the lonely chimney of Kit Hill Great Consols, the mine peopled now only by the ghosts of its long-dead miners. To the south the rivers head towards the sea and open out into broad estuaries which feel the regular pulse of the tide's ebb and flow. Eastward is the long valley of the Tamar, winding its way from north Cornwall between steep wooded cliffs and acres of market gardens to its own great estuary glittering in the distance, spanned by the twin lifelines of road and rail bridges. This is a country of winding valleys and old bridges, of woods and good farming land.

Now for a contrast as we step to the north-west and Cornwall's highest point, the summit of Brown Willy. Around us now is a sombre quiet, the brooding silence of Bodmin Moor with the colours on the downs and hills subtly changing as the clouds pass. Away to the north is the grandeur of the cliffs of north Cornwall, rising hundreds of feet above the Atlantic surf. To the west, beyond the broad sweep of the Moor, Cornwall stretches far away to lose itself in the distant haze.

From this view of nature on the grand scale, we move from one granite area to another, to the hill-top churchyard of St Dennis on the edge of Hensbarrow Downs. To the south is a bizarre landscape, the world turned inside out, the land of china clay. Human activity has radically altered the landscape but it is not without a strange beauty of its own. To the north little has changed, though now the main road runs across the open space of the Goss Moor; the hills of Belowda Beacon and Castle-an-Dinas still dominate the skyline, while away to the west the sun sparkles on the sea rolling its surf on the long beaches of the north coast.

Step now over the miles to the southern tip of the Roseland peninsula, where Zone Point reaches out into the deep blue of the English Channel. St Anthony lighthouse keeps its winking watch over the entrance to the estuary of the Fal, and from our vantage point we look across to Pendennis Castle perched above Falmouth. Inland stretches the safe anchorage of Carrick Roads; from here the tide flows to numerous tiny creeks, up to the forgotten ports on the River Fal, past the woods of Tregothnan to the wharves at Truro, whose cathedral spires look down on Georgian terraces. Away to the west curves the coastline, past the entrance to the secluded Helford River, around to the fishing coves and rugged cliffs of the Lizard peninsula. With steady wingbeats a cormorant pursues its purposeful flight a foot or so above the slight swell of the sea; out in the bay an ocean-going vessel rides at anchor, and a gentle breeze fills the sails of a hundred yachts cruising on the tranquil waters of the estuary.

A complete change awaits us as our next step brings us to the summit of Carn Brea. On this boulder-strewn height men of the vanished past set up a hill-fortification. Now we look down on the heart of Cornwall's mining district, beating less strongly now than in the eighteenth and nineteenth centuries. Numerous ruined engine-houses bear witness to this tin and copper world. Beyond the industrial scene is the line of the north cliffs, with St Agnes Beacon to the north heaving its shoulders clothed with a mantle of gorse and heather above the coastal plateau.

Finally a short step to the west and we are on yet another hill-top fortress, Trencrom Hill. In one direction St Ives Bay spreads its curve of sand; only a few miles to the south the cliffs of Mount's Bay retreat to the distant Lizard Point, and beyond the hills to the west spreads the mysterious granite world of West Penwith. Here are the monuments of the past at every turn, a sinister land of standing stones, ancient circles and the burial chambers of long-dead chieftains. Ten miles over the horizon the cliffs stand as a bastion to the Atlantic surge, and, as a medieval bishop of Exeter wrote of this extremity of his diocese, 'beyond, nothing but the great sundering Flood'.

It is tempting to think of Cornwall as depicted in travel posters—a county where the sun continually shines on golden beaches and picturesque harbours. This is one side of the picture, but a peninsula stretching out so boldly south-west towards the Atlantic cannot expect (or survive on) an endless succession of sunny days. The county has a generous quota of days when sea-mists wrap the coast and veils of rain sweep relentlessly over valley and moor, drenching the land and brimming the rivers. One can walk in the country on a placid day in spring and feel that this tranquillity is the normal way of things, but then one's eye is arrested by the sight of a thorn bush growing jaggedly on a slant. Its bent and twisted branches given an ominous hint of the great gales of winter which roar over the peninsula, carrying the sea-spray far inland.

Yet this is no less a picture of the 'real' Cornwall, where the sky and the light are an integral part of the landscape. Cornwall as we see it today bears the marks of many generations, but much of the natural landscape is part of our common heritage linking us with those generations. Our moorland hills, wooded estuaries and granite cliffs were the Cornwall of the eighteenth-century miners whose hearts were warmed by the fire of John Wesley, of the sixteenth-century rebels who defied the English Prayer Book, or earlier generations who toiled to build Norman castles, gathered by the water's edge to hear the preaching of the Celtic saints or took refuge within the ramparts of hill-top fortifications. Like ourselves, these generations lowered their heads against the storm-cloud and the gale, but also rejoiced in the freshness of a spring morning or the majesty of the sunset over the western sea.

ONE

Launceston and the South-East

The modern traveller to Cornwall following the A30 from Okehampton is now whisked into the country along a fast road and directed westward towards Bodmin. Launceston, the ancient gateway to Cornwall, which formerly commanded the road, now stands aside from the highway. Such is the way of our time.

How different it would have seemed in medieval days. The traveller making his way through Devon would arrive at the crest of the hill leading down to the Tamar, and ahead of him—seen perhaps silhouetted against the sunset—would be the unmistakable outline of Dunheved Castle. Gathered around it on the ridge, a Cornish acropolis, he would find the little town which was to be the county town of Cornwall until 1835. Beyond lay the trackless wilderness of Bodmin Moor, skirted by roads leading west. Pilgrims ventured farther on their way to St Michael's Mount in the far west, but it was not until the eighteenth century that the judges could be induced to travel more than the mile into the county which brought them to Launceston.

For the origins of this historic town we must go north of the present town to the village of St Stephens, with its fine fifteenth-century church tower. Here a monastery was established, and the name of Launceston derived from Lan Stephan (lan—a sacred enclosure). Around the ecclesiastical centre a community grew, with a weekly market. At the bottom of the hill south of this settlement the River Kensey makes its way east to join the Tamar, and it was on the opposite hill that a challenge appeared to the monastic control of the area.

After the Norman Conquest Launceston was among the estates

granted to Robert, Count of Mortain, half-brother of the Conqueror. The hill of Dunheved became a natural choice for the site of a castle, and the military settlement attracted the development of a town. When the market was moved, the future growth of Launceston by its castle was decided. The monastic centre also moved; in 1136 the new Augustinian Priory was established beside the river, and a few remains survive, though the principal remainder of the richest monastery in Cornwall is the Norman archway of polyphant stone now to be seen at the White Hart Hotel. Near the site of the priory is the church of St Thomas containing the largest Norman font in the county, perhaps a legacy from the priory church.

Medieval Launceston centred on the castle. The hill, its natural advantages increased by an artificial mound, still dominates the town, though the castle buildings are now a romantic ruin. What survives of the Norman building dates probably from the twelfth and thirteenth centuries, the principal structure being the keep. This is approached up a steep flight of steps, and consisted of a shell tower enclosing an inner keep, roofed over and containing two storeys. Lower down the hill are the south gate and the pointed vault of the north gate, alongside which is the fourteenth-century building long used as a prison. This is the notorious Doomsdale, one of whose unwilling occupants was the Quaker George Fox; his diary contains a graphic description of his harrowing experience here in 1655.

In medieval times the town was protected by walls, and the South Gate survives as a reminder of these defences. There are many buildings of character in the town (we must not forget it was for many years the county town) and in particular a sequence of fine Georgian town houses in Castle Street. But the most historic building in the town takes us back to the early sixteenth century—the parish church of St Mary Magdalene. The tower we now see is part of the fourteenth-century church which occupied the site; a vestry connects this tower with the nave, though for many years a pair of cottages filled the space. The body of the church was rebuilt on a grand scale between 1511 and 1524. What chiefly catches the eye is the carving of the exterior, all the more remarkable considering that it is entirely constructed of granite. Traditionally the church is the work of Henry Trecarrel of the nearby parish of Lezant, who was rebuilding his house at Trecarrel when his young son tragically died, and so he devoted the remainder of his material and resources to the church at Launceston. There is hardly an inch of space on the outer walls without decoration—coats of arms, foliage or figures such as St Martin or St George. At the east end is St Mary Magdalene herself reclining in a niche, flanked by musicians, and surmounting the east window the Royal Arms of Henry VIII.

Like most town churches the interior has been somewhat Victorianized, but is nevertheless fine; though never completed, it is still spacious. The eighteenth century is represented by the Royal Arms of George I, the organ front and the grand memorial to Granville Piper and Richard Wise. Much of the woodwork is modern, including the roof, screen and bench-ends, but the most prized possession is the unique pulpit. With its splendid carving it is undoubtedly the finest in Cornwall, and the recent restoration revealed the original pre-Reformation paint, surviving intact under subsequent layers.

A mile east of Launceston the Kensey reaches the end of its ten-mile journey to the Tamar. Its course brings it close to Egloskerry, whose church preserves some Norman remains. North of the village is the seventeenth-century manor house of Penheale, with a first-floor gallery, panelling and plaster-work, a magnificent wooden screen in the hall and beautiful Caroline stables. In addition to this fine work of a previous age is the extension on the south side built between the two wars by Sir Edwin Lutyens. This consists of a bold block with bay windows rather in the style of the same architect's grand work at Castle Drogo overlooking the Teign valley in Devon. Lutyens captured the spirit of the original building, so that the whole complex, including the formal garden with its cut hedges, is one of the most distinguished in Cornwall.

From Penheale the land slopes northwards to the Ottery, which rises in the lonely parish of Otterham, and eventually flows parallel to the Kensey and joins the Tamar a mile or so to the north. In its earlier reaches, however, it has to find its way around the extensive hill which is crowned with Warbstow Bury. This is a massive earthwork with double ramparts, commanding views for miles to the east and north and obviously an important defensive position. By the time the Tamar meets these tributaries just north of Launceston it has already run a large part of its course. As we have seen, it rises close to the north coast, receiving contributions from streams on either shore, and for the most part acting as the county boundary.

One of the best salmon rivers in the west country, the Tamar is spanned by several bridges, some of considerable antiquity. East of Launceston is Polston Bridge, for centuries the principal entrance to Cornwall, though the present structure only dates from the mid-nineteenth century. This way passed the Black Prince when entering Cornwall in 1354, and it was the scene for the advance and retreat of armies in the Civil War. In our time it witnessed the regular advance and retreat of tourists at summer weekends until the recent building of a new road. A few miles south, when the river has rounded the parish of Lawhitton and is broadening out, the road from Launceston to Tavistock crosses it at Greyston Bridge. This is a magnificent survival from the fifteenth century; originally the tracks approaching the bridge plunged steeply down the hill on either side, but the modern roads take an easier course in negotiating the slopes.

Much of the course of the Tamar below Greyston Bridge takes it on a very winding route, frequently doubling back on itself in arcs and loops as if to make the most of the beautiful country through which it flows. And for most of the way, until it broadens out into its estuary, its course lies in a deep valley, the slopes, often wooded, climbing steeply on either side. Three miles or so below Greyston Bridge it winds its way through extensive woods and meets its principal Cornish tributary, the Inny.

The main A30 road between Launceston and Bodmin crosses the Inny and its own tributary at Two Bridges, formerly taking a route to the north through Polyphant. Here are the quarries producing the stone named after the village, a blue-grey stone which polishes well and is used in Truro Cathedral and not surprisingly in the local parish church of Lewannick, perched on its hill. This church contains two stones with carved inscriptions, partly in Latin and partly in the Ogham script of southern Ireland. There is also a cresset stone, a rare example of this type of lighting. With the tallow filling the seven holes, representing the seven sacraments, alight, the atmosphere in the darkened church must have been marvellously solemn and mysterious.

The Inny flows on through the parish of Lezant, close to the home of Henry Trecarrel, the benefactor of Launceston (and traditionally of other churches in the district). This is a remarkable medieval survival. The chapel was originally built at the beginning of the fifteenth century, an example of a private chapel licensed for the use of a family living at a distance from the parish church. The existing granite chapel dates from the early sixteenth century, and nearby the hall of the manor house also survives, after Cotehele the finest medieval hall in Cornwall.

Greyston Bridge dates from 1439, when an Indulgence was granted to those contributing to its building. Two years earlier a similar Indulgence had been granted to raise funds for the building of Horse Bridge, a few miles downstream. This carried the road from Tavistock to Liskeard and south Cornwall, and at that time was the lowest crossing of the river. The road climbs from the river to the village of Stoke Climsland with its stately granite church tower. Here too is the Duchy Home Farm, though there are also several reminders that this was the northern edge of a mining area.

At Horse Bridge the Tamar flows through meadows, but a few miles further on it enters a wooded gorge and is spanned by the seven arches of New Bridge. This bridge is new by comparison with Horse Bridge, being built about a hundred years later and affording a more direct route from Tavistock to Liskeard. Indeed until recently it was the lowest road bridge on the river, though ferries connected south-east Cornwall with Plymouth.

The Devon bank of the gorge is thickly wooded, but the road on the Cornish side climbs through the hillside village of Gunnislake to the ridgeway leading west to Callington. There is plenty of evidence here of the mining which was formerly the principal activity of the district. The bulk of the Cornish mining area lies in the west of the county, but there was mineral wealth here also around the granite outcrops of Hingston Down and Kit Hill, which rises to dominate the area.

Below New Bridge, which like Polston Bridge proved itself of strategic value in the Civil War, the Tamar meets tidal water and follows a winding course under wooded cliffs, past the restored quay at Morwellham on the Devon bank and round to the little river port of Calstock. Here the river is spanned by the twelve slender arches of a viaduct carrying the railway 120 feet above the water from Plymouth to Gunnislake. In 1872 the East Cornwall Mineral Railway operated a line connecting the quarries and mines of the area with Calstock Quay, which was reached by a cable-operated incline. In 1891 the line was taken over by the Plymouth, Devonport and South-Western Junction Railway, and the viaduct was constructed; until 1934 wagons were raised from the quay to the viaduct by means of a lift. The line was opened in 1908, and, though designed to serve the mines and quarries, later also supplied transport facilities for the market-garden produce of the Tamar valley. Formerly the line ran as far as Kit Hill and Kelly Bray, near Callington, but the section beyond Gunnislake closed in 1966.

Below Calstock the Tamar turns south and passes the woods of Cotehele where survives the finest manor house in the late medieval tradition in the west country. The house came to the Edgcumbe family by marriage in 1353, and some alterations were subsequently made, but the main building took place between 1485 and 1539, the work of Sir Richard Edgcumbe and his son Sir Piers.

It was not until the accession of Henry Tudor brought some stability to the turbulent fifteenth century that Sir Richard's work began. After his death in 1489 Sir Piers continued the building work: the great hall is his principal achievement. The building we see today was completed when the tower was constructed in 1627, associated with a Dutch merchant, Sir Thomas Coteele—the similarity of name is apparently pure coincidence—whose daughter married into the Edgcumbe family and who as a result lived here for a time. At some time in the late seventeenth century the family moved into their other home at Mount Edgcumbe, overlooking Plymouth Sound, a house very much in the modern fashion when it was built at the beginning of the reign of Elizabeth.

The fact that Cotehele remained in the possession of the family but was not their principal residence explains its survival undamaged and intact. It was preserved and maintained, but the enlargement which for residential requirements would have been considered essential was not necessary here. It is now in the care of the National Trust, who acquired it in 1947 by a method which set a precedent: the Treasury accepted it in settlement of death duties, and handed it over to the Trust. As a result the house may be seen, together with its collection of seventeenth- and eighteenth-century furnishings.

Sir Richard's work is seen first in the large barn beside the main approach and then in the gatehouse through which we enter the Hall Court. From this court an archway leads to the Retainers' Court, the two quadrangles giving the impression of a small college. In the corner of the Hall Court is the perpendicular east window of Sir Richard's chapel; this was considerably restored in the last century, but retains much of its original glass, barrel roof and oak screen. In the corner of the chapel is a clock dating from Sir Richard's time, unaltered and still in working order. Until the beginning of this century the bell in its little moulded granite bell-cote regularly sounded the hours over the estate as it had done since the dawn of the Tudor period.

We enter the house through the Hall, built with a traditional medieval roof by Sir Piers Edgcumbe, and unusual in having no screens passage as is normally found in a hall of this type. The walls are hung with armour and weaponry which preserve the atmosphere of the period. Beyond the hall is the kitchen and the small enclosed kitchen court at the heart of the house. Tapestries cover the walls of the smaller rooms, such as the Old Dining Room and the neighbouring Punch Room which gives access to the seventeenth-century tower in the north-west corner of the house. The bedrooms above these rooms and in the tower contain splendid four-poster beds and furniture mainly from the seventeenth century. In the Staircase Lobby is an unusual piece of Welsh furniture, the Cotehele Tester, an early sixteenth-century bedhead which seems to have come to the house at the time of Sir Piers' marriage to a Welsh widow in 1532.

On a commanding site north of the house is a three-sided tower, probably of late eighteenth-century date and perhaps built in commemoration of the visit of George III and his family in the summer of 1789. In spring the banks are bright with daffodils, and at all seasons there is a sense of tranquillity and intimacy. Few places retain the romantic medieval charm which lingers within the grey courts of this manor house set in its woods above the winding Tamar.

The river passes Cotehele Quay, with Halton Quay two miles further to the south. In earlier times the river was the principal means of communication for the area and vital for the movement of goods. The road climbs from the river to the village of St Dominick, set among the market gardens of the Tamar valley. Horticulture is an important part of the economy of the valley south of Horse Bridge, particularly on the Cornish side of the river. Flowers and fruit are the principal crops, with a smaller proportion of vegetables, and much of the produce of the area finds its way to markets in the Midlands, the North and as far as Scotland.

Following the river south in its now leisurely progress we come to St Mellion. The churchtown sits astride the main road, on high ground which falls away gradually on either hand to river valleys. In the church are the monuments of the Coryton family, who lived at Crocadon, just north of the village. From here in a previous century probably came one of Cornwall's foremost medieval writers, John of Trevisa, born in 1326, before the village church had acquired its north aisle and tower. For seven years he was a Fellow of Exeter College, Oxford, which had been founded earlier in the century by Bishop Walter Stapledon of Exeter and where so many westcountrymen over the years studied. Later he was at Queen's College, but then left Oxford to enter the service of the fourth Lord Berkeley as chaplain and vicar of Berkeley in Gloucestershire, where he died in 1412.

A remarkable linguist (whose native tongue was Cornish), it was as a translator of Latin works into English that John of Trevisa made a reputation, his prose writings being contemporaneous with the work of Chaucer. According to tradition he helped in Wycliffe's translation of the Bible, but his most notable work lay in translating the *Polychronicon* of Ranulf Higden, a Benedictine monk of Chester. This appeared in 1387, and consisted of a comprehensive history, the most exhaustive to have then appeared, and valuable for its information on the historical, scientific and geographical knowledge of that time; the translator brought the history up to date and added some notes for good measure.

A mile or two to the south-east is Pentillie Castle, whose woods border the Tamar as it winds round in a last sweeping loop before finally turning seawards and broadening out to its estuary. The castle, now for the most part unfortunately demolished, was built early in the nineteenth century by William Wilkins, incorporating a seventeenth-century wing which survives. An eccentric member of the family, Sir James Tillie, was buried a century earlier in a tower built as a folly at Mount Ararat on the north of the estate. His wish was that his embalmed body should be seated in the upper room of the tower: if he was reluctant to forsake the splendid view over the Tamar, one can sympathize.

From Paynter's Cross where there is a delightful Regency estate office, the road runs down to the riverside parish of Landulph. In the fifteenth century there was a flourishing port here, supplying five ships for the nation's use in the Hundred Years' War. The main centre of population is at Cargreen, with its quay for yachtsmen facing across the water to Devon. The church is tucked away down its lane and preserves some old work, particularly bench-ends carved with animal figures. There are monuments to the Lower family of Clifton in the north of the parish where the river winds its final loop, and also a brass commemorating Theodore Palaeologus. This sounds the most unlikely person to turn up in this remote corner of Cornwall, the last descendant of the medieval Christian emperors of Byzantium, but it was at Clifton that he died in January 1636 and in Landulph church is his last resting place.

The church faces south to the two bridges which span the river between Saltash and the Devon shore. The ancient town of Saltash was granted its charter in 1190 and for a long time was a fishing port strategically situated at a narrow part of the estuary and claiming jurisdiction over its tidal reaches. This was in the days before men thought in terms of bridges in the sky. Their construction has altered the character of the area, not only of Saltash itself, but of the whole of south-east Cornwall which looks increasingly towards Plymouth.

By its geographical situation facing the Devon shore, and particularly with the developing importance of Plymouth and Devonport, the passage across the Tamar has always been of importance to Saltash. There was a ferry here in early medieval times, as there was downstream at Cremyll connecting with Stonehouse. A steam floating bridge was introduced in 1829, a few years before the similar link at Torpoint which is still in regular use. But in 1833 an appointment was made which was later to have a profound effect on Saltash: the Great Western Railway appointed as their chief engineer Isambard Kingdom Brunel.

Several stretches of railway line were in operation in Cornwall before the plan to bridge the Tamar was considered. This new development altered the whole conception of travel between Cornwall and the rest of the country. Work on the line between Saltash and Truro involved the construction of a large number of viaducts, the highest at St Pinnock near Liskeard and the longest, 443 yards, at Truro. Originally the stone pillars were surmounted by fan-shaped wooden trellises which carried the track, wood being cheaper. However, wooden trellises were not only a fire hazard—tanks of water were kept at each end—but were costly to maintain, and the timber was gradually replaced by stone. Another conversion programme was the change from Brunel's broad gauge to narrow; when this took place in May 1892 it meant that through trains from the North and Midlands could come right into Cornwall.

The Royal Albert Bridge project was the most problematical task faced at that date. A double-span bridge was necessary, and Brunel devised the unusual structure which we now see, the drag of the chains balancing the thrust of the tubular arches. Gradually the two spans of 455 feet were raised into position, 100 feet above the water, and on 2 May 1859 the Prince Consort officially opened the bridge named in his honour. In addition to the curves of its construction, the bridge itself curves across the water. It is not only a construction of beauty but an engineering masterpiece.

A century was to pass before the next development. It had been apparent for some time that the road links between Devon and Cornwall were inadequate, and eventually in 1961 the toll bridge was opened to replace the ferry and create a smooth passage for the ever-increasing volume of road traffic. The solid single-arch suspension bridge makes a remarkable contrast with its old neighbour: indeed the Tamar as a whole offers an interesting study of bridges through the centuries, each of them no doubt the pride of its own time.

Inevitably the bridges dominate the town of Saltash, and the contrast between the houses by the water and the piers striding overhead is unforgettable. The town climbs up the hillside from the waterfront, through many of its old houses have now made way for modern buildings. The Town Hall, however, survives, situated near the church. Norman work in the base of the tower and the blocked south door remind us of the antiquity of this building, though only in 1881 did it become a parish church. The mother church is at St Stephen's, south-west of the town, where a large font with carvings of faces and animals is the chief Norman survival.

As the railway leaves Saltash and swings away from the Tamar it crosses a viaduct over a creek dominated by the Norman castle of Trematon, under whose protection Saltash grew. Here in addition to the oval-shaped shell keep is a fine thirteenth-century gatehouse. The hall in the inner bailey made way in the early nineteenth century for a pretty battlemented Georgian mansion, and the castle remains a private residence. In the late sixteenth or early seventeenth century another castle, Ince, was built not far away for the rising Killigrew family. Ince is actually a fortified house, a square, symmetrical brick building with slate-hung square towers at each corner, covered with pyramidal roofs. Its charm is greatly enhanced by its situation away from the roads and overlooking the river with woods on the opposite shore.

The river over which both Trematon and Ince Castles command a view is no longer the Tamar but the estuary to which a number of rivers contribute, principally the Lynher. This joins the Tamar below Saltash. South-east Cornwall is an area of estuaries, the incoming tide flowing over the mud-flats and extending innumerable winding fingers up wooded valleys. The Lynher itself rises on the north-eastern side of Bodmin Moor, flowing round the eastern flank of the Moor and heading south on a journey of 30 miles to the broad waters of the estuary. Few rivers are as beautiful as the tranquil Lynher, shaded by trees reflected in its salmon-rich water.

The tide flows as far as Notter Bridge where the road from Saltash swoops downhill and up to Landrake on the way to Liskeard. The village of Landrake sits on the top of its hill, so that its 100 foot tower is a landmark for many miles. Above Pillaton the river flows under Clapper Bridge, which is now a misnomer. A clapper bridge consists of huge slabs of granite laid on piles of boulders forming a rough but sturdy crossing, such as can be found on the De Lank river on Bodmin Moor. This bridge in its beautiful setting was rebuilt in the sixteenth century with three arches, but retained its earlier name.

Following the wooded course of the Lynher upstream we pass the partly ruined Queen Anne house of Newton Ferrers, and skirt the hill crowned with the prehistoric earthwork of Cadson Bury before reaching Newbridge. Like its namesake at Gunnislake it is only new by comparision with existing medieval bridges; in fact it is probably about 50 years older than the Gunnislake bridge. Rebuilding has been necessary at times, but the bridge is still basically of fifteenth-century work with heavy granite piers and four round arches. It carries the road from Gunnislake to Liskeard, and three miles to the west is the hamlet of St Ive, the churchtown of the mining village of Pensilva. St Ive church is unusual in having a good deal of fourteenth-century work, notably in the chancel; traditionally the sixteenth-century tower is among the benefactions of Henry Trecarrel of Lezant.

East of Newbridge the road climbs steeply to the small town of Callington, dominated by Kit Hill to the north-east. South of the town is the little baptistery of Dupath Well, a granite building dating probably from the fifteenth century. Water runs into a basin and out again at the back. A gabled roof covers the building, complete with a granite bellcote.

For many years the mother church of the town was at South Hill, three miles away to the north-west, a building rigorously restored but preserving an inscribing stone from the sixth or seventh century with a Chi-Rho monogram. Callington church itself, a fine fifteenth-century building, has recovered somewhat from its own restoration. Many Cornish churches suffered at the hands of the Victorian 'restorers'; in the words of Sir John Betjeman,

> *The Church's Restoration*
> *In eighteen-eighty-three*
> *Has left for contemplation*
> *Not what there used to be.*

To be fair, it is true that many buildings were on the point of collapse and would not have survived without drastic action. However, tact and sensitivity did not always play much of a part.

Leaving the higher reaches of the Lynher for the time being, we shall return to the estuary by way of the little River Tiddy, a few miles to the west. Rising on the mine-scarred slopes of Caradon Hill, its southward course brings it to the farming parish of Quethiock. The village is approached by winding lanes, and has a church with a saddleback roof and an unusually narrow west tower. When the restoration was necessary here in 1878, much of the work was done by the vicar of the time whose handiwork can be seen in woodcarving and stained glass.

The river bustles on its way and is crossed by the busy road from Saltash to Liskeard at Tideford, which, despite the name of the river, pronounces itself as two syllables. In fact the tide does flow almost as far as the village, and the river broadens out as it approaches the estuary. On the west bank is the estate of Port Eliot with its beech woods, the park being laid out by Humphry Repton at the end of the eighteenth century. Parts of the house are early eighteenth-century, but for the most part it was rebuilt at the beginning of the nineteenth century by Sir John Soane, notably the castellated east front.

In the early seventeenth century this was the home of the great champion of Parliamentary rights, Sir John Eliot, who earned the displeasure of Charles I by forcing him to accept the Petition of Right and leading the attack on Buckingham. Despite the Petition of Right, Eliot was imprisoned in the Tower and died there, a few days after he had had his portait painted. This portrait of a sickly but determined man is at the house, though his body did not return to Cornwall: Charles turned down the request of his son with the words, 'Let Sir John Eliot be buried in the church of that parish where he died'.

Eliot had sat in Parliament as member for St Germans, which we see today with its church adjoining the house of Port Eliot, its picturesque group of six gabled almshouses and its quay at the mouth of the Tiddy. The ecclesiastical history of St Germans takes us back well before the Norman Conquest to the day when Athelstan brought Cornwall under English administration and the Celtic Church accepted the authority of the Roman tradition. A Cornish see was established at St Germans in 931 and lasted until 1043 when it was moved to Crediton; seven years later the joint see was transferred to Exeter, and Cornwall remained an archdeaconry in a vast diocese covering the two western counties until the nineteenth century.

Meanwhile at St Germans the monastery was reconstituted in the late twelfth century as a Priory of Augustinian canons, and a new church was built. Its west front remains the finest specimen of Norman architecture in the county, simple and grand. The twin towers are surmounted by contrasting upper stages of a later date, but the lower stages are original. Between them is the west doorway with seven orders; the stonework—elvan from the Tartan Down quarry at Landrake—has suffered from the ravages of centuries of westerly wind and rain, but is still powerfully impressive. So also is the effect of the interior, although it is now only a torso of what it was before the collapse of the chancel in 1592 and the pulling down of the north aisle. There are several Morris windows, including a Burne-Jones east window. By the time of the Dissolution the number of canons was small; the Champernowne family acquired the monastic estate and later sold it to the Plymouth merchant John Eliot in whose family it has remained. As at Trematon the contrast between the classical lines of the Georgian mansion and the austerity of the medieval building is striking.

St Germans Quay lies at the head of the estuary, but before exploring its southern shore we shall go further west to follow the course of another river, the Seaton. Like the Tiddy it rises in the mining country south-east of Bodmin Moor, but unlike its eastern neighbour it pursues an independent course to the south coast. After flowing close to the town of Liskeard it reaches the parish of

Menheniot with its farms and quarries. The village can be distinguished from a distance because of the sharply pointed spire of its church, which preserves the earliest brass in the county, dated 1386.

From Menheniot the river enters the valley below Catchfrench Manor where more of Humphry Repton's landscaping work took place, and then follows a thickly wooded course past the village of Hessenford and south to the sea. Here at the village of Seaton the river spreads over the pebbly beach at the end of its journey. From Hessenford the main road from Looe makes for the south-east corner of the country, and the same destination can be reached by a coast road from Seaton. This route takes us past the bungalows of Downderry to Crafthole and the former fishing village of Portwrinkle, now a holiday cove. From here the coast sweeps eastwards in the long curve of Whitesand Bay, guarded in the distance by the bulk of Rame Head.

Inland from Crafthole the main road passes through Sheviock on its way to the ferry at Torpoint, though the medieval track would have followed the southern route to Cremyll. We are now back on the southern side of the Lynher, and two or three miles further on the church of Antony stands well up to survey the view down the estuary. Here are an early brass to Margery Arundell and monuments from three centuries to members of the Carew family. The present representatives of the family, like their ancestors, live at the splendid Antony House which commands the passage across the mouth of the Lynher. The Carews have been at Antony since the late fifteenth century, and the most famous member of the family was the historian Richard Carew.

Richard Carew lived through all the excitements of the Elizabethan age, but fortunately did not have to endure the tragic experience of the Civil War, which divided the family loyalties. Sir Alexander Carew defended St Nicholas Island in Plymouth Sound on behalf of Parliament, but underwent a change of heart as the war went on. However, his plan to hand over the strategically-placed island to the Royalists came to the knowledge of the Parliamentarians: as a result he was executed as a traitor. His brother John was not troubled by any doubts as to the right side to support; his opposition to the King was total, and execution came to him also, in his case in 1660 as a regicide. Sir Alexander's grandson Sir William Carew was a convinced Stuart supporter, but ironically this too brought trouble, since it led to his arrest in 1715

as a Jacobite sympathizer. Nevertheless the present house was
built during his time, being completed in 1721, and was given to
the National Trust in 1961.

Tradition credits James Gibbs with the design of Antony; it is
certainly in his style and is undeniably the finest classical country
house of its date in Cornwall. Built of light grey Pentewan stone,
it is approached from a forecourt flanked by brick arcades and
cupolas. The house itself is beautifully proportioned with an air of
simplicity and dignity; the gardens extend on the north side with
fine views across the Lynher. A granite *porte-cochère* was added to
the south front in the mid-nineteenth century, and through this
approach we enter the house.

Much of the furniture is contemporary with the house itself,
and there are several paintings of interest. The hall is dominated
by Edward Bower's portrait of Charles I, a study of the King at
his trial which captures his dignity on that occasion. In the library is a painting of Sir Alexander Carew: stitches at the bottom
remind us that when he showed himself an active supporter of the
Parliamentarian cause the portrait was hacked from its frame by
Royalist members of the family, but at his martyrdom—as they
regarded his death—the portrait was restored with honour.

Also in the hall is a portrait of Richard Carew, the Tudor historian of Cornwall; he appears as he was in 1586, High Sheriff of
the county at the age of 32. He was also a member of Parliament,
but his achievements were not in the field of public life or military
exploits so much as in that of scholarship. As one of the gentry he
had time to devote to his many interests; he was master of five
languages, and translated several works from Spanish and Italian.
The *Survey of Cornwall* occupied him during the last decade of the
sixteenth century, and was published in 1602. Not only is it enter-
taining in its own right, but it gives us an invaluable look at the
topography and industries of the country, a picture of late
Elizabethan Cornwall seen through the eyes of an intelligent and
observant country gentleman.

East of Antony House is the mid-Victorian church of Merifield,
formerly the estate church, and from here the road brings us down
into Torpoint. The town has grown almost entirely since the
introduction of the ferry to Devonport across the Hamoaze, as this
stretch of the Tamar estuary is known. The southern part of the
peninsula is occupied by naval training establishments, and
beyond these a road leads south through the little village of St

John to Millbrook at the head of its tidal lake.

To the south of Millbrook the road climbs the hill to Maker Heights and the church on the edge of the Mount Edgcumbe estate. The landscaped park makes a splendid contribution to the scenery of Plymouth Sound, and is particularly impressive seen from the Hoe, with Drake's Island in the foreground. The road skirts the estate down to the ferry passage at Cremyll, which has certainly existed since the thirteenth century, and to the south are the twin fishing villages of Kingsand and Cawsand. These villages adjoin each other and face across to the Devon shore, sheltered by the high ground behind them. To maintain unified administration of the strategically important Plymouth Sound, Kingsand was in Devon until 1844, when the parish of Maker was transferred to Cornwall.

From Cawsand we can follow the footpath along the wooded slope overlooking Plymouth Sound until we reach the south-eastern extremity at Penlee Point. Here the coastline turns abruptly westward for two miles, interrupted by Rame Head thrusting its conical bulk out into the English Channel before we find ourselves at the eastern end of Whitesand Bay. On the hill is the remote church of Rame, raising its broach spire bravely against the wind.

The chapel on Rame Head is dedicated to St Michael. The archangel, Cornwall's patron saint, is particularly associated with high places, and we shall find other sites in the county under his protection. A narrow neck of land joins the mainland to the promontory, once the site of a cliff castle, and from its summit the bracken-covered slopes fall away to the sea. To the east are the shores of Devon on the farther side of Plymouth Sound, away to the west the headlands of the south Cornish coast with the Lizard 50 miles distant on the horizon. And to the south the spread of the English Channel where the great ships go, ocean liners and oil tankers, on the same waters where on a July day in 1588 the proud crescent of galleons advanced eastward and England's destiny hung in the balance.

TWO

The North-East
and Bodmin Moor

Let us return from the mouth of the Tamar to its source 60 miles or so to the north. It is only a matter of yards from here to the source of another stream which turns west and chatters down between the wooded hills which open to the sea at Marsland Mouth. Here as on Maker Heights or Rame Head we look across the water to Devon, here again the Cornwall coastal footpath sets out on its journey, and again we can gaze out at the sea which has so powerfully influenced Cornwall and the Cornish.

But there the similarity ends. The south-east and the north-east corners of the county offer a sharp contrast in coastal scenery. As we stand on Rame Head we watch the shipping in the Channel, boats making for the welcoming fishing ports or the waters of Plymouth Sound with all its human activity. Not so at Marsland Mouth. Here is no friendly harbour to offer shelter to boats. The dark cliffs face west to defy the might of the Atlantic surge, and wicked fangs of rock stretch out into the surf.

From Padstow Point to Lundy Light
Is a watery grave by day or night

runs the old rhyme, and shipping gives this coast a wide berth; the little stream flows quietly out to lose itself on the stony shore, and the cliffs rise lonely and grand on either side, facing the sunset.

The parish occupying this northerly extremity of Cornwall is Morwenstow, distinguished not only by its geographical position but by some of the most magnificent coastal scenery in the whole of the west. A road leads down from the little village to the church, standing above a deep valley where a stream hurries down to the sea. The church is notable not only for its situation, but for the Norman work which has survived. Solid circular pillars support a north arcade, and a Norman south doorway also survives, moved to its present position when a south aisle was added in the fifteenth century. The spirit of the past lingers here, and there is a sense of mystery within the building, accentuated by the contrast with the natural world outside.

The National Trust owns the land between the church and Vicarage Cliff to the south; the footpath takes us past the church, westward towards the sea. From the cliff top the views are breathtaking: to the south Higher Sharpnose Point reaches out into the sea, the first of a succession of headlands which lead the eye miles along the coast; the dramatic bulk of Henna Cliff rises to the north, while far beyond it Lundy Island lies on the horizon. And always below us the Atlantic surges around the black rocks stretching out from the foot of these tremendous cliffs.

High above the sea at Vicarage Cliff is a hut built from driftwood, a relic of the last century and of the man whose name is now inseparably linked with Morwenstow—Robert Stephen Hawker. In 1834 he became vicar in what was then an extremely remote and isolated parish, and remained until his death in 1875. Shortly after his arrival he built the vicarage which we see today on the slope of the valley below the church; its chimneys resemble church towers which he had known in his earlier years, a stroke of individualism characteristic of the man.

Hawker accepted the living willingly, but found his task daunting, since relations were never easy between the parishioners and their Tractarian vicar. It was perhaps this isolation combined with the desolate nature of the parish which helped to turn him into an eccentric. And this is the image which has survived: a figure clad in a fisherman's jersey and sea-boots striding around the wind-blown parish, dreaming visions and writing poems such as *The Song of the Western Men* and *The Quest of the Sangraal*.

He was a devoted parish priest, and the restoration of the church, with the rebuilding of the rood screen, was his work. He was particularly concerned when storms swept ships on to the rocks, and as a man of profound sensibility these tragic scenes were agonizing for him. On many occasions he played a leading part in the grim task of recovering corpses from the sea, and numbers of sailors lie buried in the churchyard.

As a writer Hawker achieved early success as a winner of the

Newdigate Poetry Prize at Oxford. He was one of the best minor poets of the Victorian age, particularly good as a ballad writer. Much of his poetry took shape as he brooded in the dark sanctuary of his church or within the ships' timbers of his eyrie on the cliffs; it is here that we can best recapture his spirit, especially when the gales are high and the sea thunders savagely against the gaunt cliffs.

Following the road south from Morwenstow we pass the entrance to Tonacombe Manor, a miniature beauty of a medieval and Tudor house, with panelled rooms and a minstrels' gallery. As we reach the top of the hill the heights of Bodmin Moor stand up unmistakably in the distance, over 20 miles away; more immediately in front of us the landscape is dominated by the two huge saucer-like aerials of the Composite Signals Organisation Station, part of the international communications system linked by satellite. A steep descent brings us to the Coombe Valley, where a stream reaches the sea at Duckpool, the little beach sheltering in the lee of Steeple Point. The cliff is National Trust land and so is the beautiful Coombe Valley itself, where wooded hills rise on either hand as the stream approaches the sea.

The road climbing the hill to the south of the valley passes Stowe Barton, whose solid walls shelter a long seventeenth-century farmhouse. This is all that now survives to remind us of the Grenvilles of Stowe, the family which dominated this part of Cornwall and north Devon, producing such notable figures as Sir Richard Grenville of the *Revenge* who perished 'at Flores in the Azores', and Sir Bevil Grenville who fell at the battle of Lansdown in 1643. The family monuments are in their parish church at Kilkhampton, a village a couple of miles inland, set astride the main ridgeway road following the watershed into north Devon.

Like Morwenstow, Kilkhampton church possesses a fine Norman south doorway, but in other respects provides a contrast with its northern neighbour. Morwenstow crouches low against the hillside, with an atmosphere of solemnity; Kilkhampton stands up proudly, and is quite large for a Cornish church. It has a fine collection of sixteenth-century bench-ends, while the organ incorporates the original work of Father Smith.

Bench-ends are a characteristic of several churches in this area. Another feature of this part of Cornwall worth noting is the number of non-Cornish names. The Anglo-Saxon settlement made a greater impact here than further west, and the place-names naturally reflect this influence. As we advance further from the Devon border, so the Cornish names grow more numerous, and in the far west the names are almost exclusively Cornish.

The main road through Kilkhampton takes us south towards Stratton and Bude, the main centre of population in this northern part of the county. The ancient town of Stratton rises on the hillside above the River Neet, and is on the course of a Roman road which entered Cornwall in this north-eastern corner. The church presides over some pleasant Georgian and older buildings. The former manor house, now an inn, was the birthplace of Anthony Payne, the giant retainer of Sir Bevil Grenville, who stood over seven feet high; he died here and now lies buried in the churchyard.

A modern statue of St Andrew looks down at us from the west tower of the church, and in the porch is preserved the old door of the prison with the ominous word 'Clink' patterned in nails across it. The building dates from various periods, the north arcade being fourteenth-century, of polyphant stone, the south arcade granite of a century later. There are two notable monuments, a fourteenth-century effigy of a knight, and a fine brass of 1561 commemorating Sir John Arundell of Trerice and his two wives. There is also good modern glass, west windows by Kempe and Tower and an east window designed by Burne-Jones.

The church preserves relics from the battle of Stamford Hill, fought in 1643 just north of the town. Passing the site of the battlefield we can approach Bude from the north, by way of the attractive little hillside village of Poughill. The church, with the unusual dedication to the Danish St Olaf, is a building of considerable charm; its wall paintings of St Christopher have been repainted with an artificial boldness, but the pride of the church is its woodwork, particularly another fine set of old bench-ends.

By comparison with these old villages, Bude is a newcomer, with little distinctively Cornish in its character. The River Neet, flowing south from Stratton, is joined at Helebridge by other streams from Jacobstow and Week St Mary, and the combined river takes a northerly course to reach the sea by a fine stretch of beach. As a harbour Bude acquired some importance when the canal was built in the early 1820's, but later in the century its trade passed to the newly-arrived railway. This in its turn brought tourists, and the holiday world of boarding houses and hotels became the leading feature of the town; as a resort it has fortunately not outgrown itself, nor has it spoilt its coast.

The railway which put paid to the canal as a commercial concern has itself now disappeared. The line formerly ran through Holsworthy to Okehampton, but this closed down, like the former line running from Launceston round the north of Bodmin Moor to Camelford and Wadebridge. Ironically the canal has partially outlasted the railway, though only the seaward mile or two is still navigable.

The purpose of the canal was to connect Launceston and Holsworthy with the north coast, the main cargoes being sand for use as a fertiliser, coal, slate and building materials. Its entrance is by the mouth of the River Neet, where a breakwater was constructed to form a basin behind the lock gates. The canal followed the course of the river inland to Helebridge, and barges were used on this section. From this point tub-boats were used, and the canal was consequently narrower. Six inclined planes were needed on the various stretches of the canal, the first at Marhamchurch where stationary steam engines drew the boats up the incline from Helebridge.

The canal as a whole was abandoned in 1891, though several parts of the system can still be made out as it snakes its way through the country following the contours. The Launceston branch of the canal follows the course of the Tamar and ends north of the town at Druxton wharf. But as with the track of the railway, nature is gradually claiming back its territory.

Hidden away down a lane not far from Stratton is the remote church of Launcells. On the hillside above the church stands an enchanting Queen Anne house, with a pretty perron, and beside the stream which runs below the church is the old holy well of St Swithin, to whom the church is dedicated. This utterly unspoilt and unchanged interior is perhaps unique in Cornwall in its atmosphere of remote sequesteredness. The walls are plastered and the windows are clear, so the interior is filled with exquisite light and we can appreciate its fine proportions. The chancel has heraldic tiles of the fifteenth century and there is a complete and splendid set of bench-ends like those at Kilkhampton and Poughill; presumably the same craftsmen produced these sets, with their similarity of style. Another skill is commemorated in Hawker's ballad, 'The Ringers of Launcells Tower': the band who rang for the accession of George III in 1760 all survived to ring at his jubilee 50 years later—and two of them even celebrated in this same tower the coronation of William IV.

> *Hark! proudly hark! with that true tone*
> *They welcomed him to land and throne;*
> *So ere they die they fain would ring*
> *The jubilee of England's king.*

In the quiet churchyard is buried Sir Goldsworthy Gurney, who died in the same year as Hawker but was a man in complete contrast: Hawker hated industrialism, Gurney advanced it. During his schooldays he witnessed one of Richard Trevithick's experiments with a steam-engine on wheels; this impressed him deeply, and profoundly influenced the course of this life. He began his working life as a surgeon at Wadebridge, but his leisure hours were devoted to studying mechanical science and chemistry. He started experiments in steam and locomotion; his purpose was to construct an engine which could travel on the public roads, and in 1829 he achieved the first long journey at a maintained speed by any locomotive. However, as a commercial endeavour his work was thwarted by government legislation against the use of steam on public roads, and so Gurney applied himself elsewhere.

His great contribution to scientific progress at this time was the development of the high pressure steam-jet, and this means of power he now applied to other uses. Among these were extinguishing fires in mines, ventilating sewers, and the Gurney stove. Then he became interested in light. In 1864 he published 'Observations pointing out a means by which a Seaman may identify Lighthouses, and know their Distance from his Ship, in any position or bearing of the Compass'. Gurney built the Castle in Bude, facing the sea between the river and the canal, now used as municipal offices, and here he spent his last years. The tablet in Poughill church records pleasantly that 'his inventions and discoveries in Steam and Electricity made communication by land and sea so rapid that it became necessary for all England to keep uniform clock time'.

From Bude the main road brings us close to the church of Poundstock, which like Launcells has a beautiful rural setting on a hillside amid trees. There are not the numbers of bench-ends to compare with Launcells but there is a good deal of old woodwork, some painted panels of an old rood screen and some interesting wall paintings; in addition, below the church is a two-storeyed medieval guild house.

The grandeur of the cliffs at Morwenstow gives way to a gentler coast near Bude, as far south as Widemouth Bay. But now we climb the heights again, and the coastal scenery from here to Tintagel is as spectacular as anywhere in the county. On high ground near the coast, but sheltering in a dip with a school and farm buildings, is the little church of St Gennys in an isolated corner of its parish. The road runs down a steep hill to the beach at Crackington Haven, where the black cliffs tower on either side of the inlet, and the folds of the rock strata are clearly visible.

The National Trust owns Pencannow Point on the east of Crackington Haven and the grand succession of cliffs for two miles to the west, beginning with the dramatically jagged headland of Cambeak. From here the coastal footpath climbs above the beach uninvitingly named The Strangles and finally reaches the summit of High Cliff, at 730 feet the loftiest cliff in the county. It does not rise sheer from the sea, and at first its height is not apparent. But when one sees the gulls wheeling far below and the waves crawling like the wrinkled sea of Tennyson's Eagle, one realises the scale of this awesome place. On goes the procession to Buckator, Beeny Cliff and Pentargon, where a stream plunges in a cascade to the rocks 80 feet below.

We are now in the parish of St Juliot, whose church lies in solitude away down a narrow lane. In the valley below the church the beautiful Valency river makes its way through shadowy woods to the sea at Boscastle. A mile or so before it reaches the little harbour the stream passes close to Minster, the mother church of Boscastle, hidden away in an exquisite leafy glen.

Nothing now remains of the Norman castle of Botreaux which once stood on the hill behind the village of Boscastle, but its existence testifies to the importance of the harbour in this cleft of the rocks on an inhospitable shore. Between the two headlands which guard the entrance the channel twists and turns, and jetties protect the harbour itself; negotiating the passage is never easy in rough weather and so it has never developed as a regular port, but over the centuries many vessels caught in storms have been grateful for its sanctuary. Thanks to the steep slopes, and now the protection of the National Trust, the village has preserved its character and charm.

On the western slopes of the village is the ancient settlement of Forrabury, its church bare and exposed above the cliffs, like its neighbour a mile down the coast at Trevalga. Both churches were Norman foundations, though little now remains from that time.

However, at Forrabury there is an even older survival, the Common, where the medieval open field pattern still exists. This is probably a legacy from Celtic times: the land is divided into strips known as 'stitches', mostly running from north to south. The tenants work their individual portions during the summer months, and during the winter the land is grazed in common.

St Juliot church has an imperishable memory, for the architect responsible for its restoration was the young Thomas Hardy. In March 1870 he made his first acquaintance with Cornwall and with the woman he was to marry. Emma Gifford, sister-in-law of the vicar, lived at the vicarage, and in fact welcomed the architect when he first arrived from Launceston. He spent his few days at St Juliot working at the church and seeing something of the neighbourhood.

Hardy married Emma four years later, but the romance failed and the marriage was not a successs. Nevertheless the experience had a powerful effect on his imagination. The first visit to St Juliot inspired his romantic novel *A Pair of Blue Eyes,* which opens with the daughter of the vicar of Endelstow in Cornwall waiting for the young architect who is coming to make plans for the restoration of the church. The novel is not an autobiography, but the visits to St Juliot, walking in the Valency valley or along the coast, laid its foundation.

Hardy the novelist was inspired by Cornwall, and even more did it influence Hardy the poet. Yet it was not until after Emma's death in 1912 that he wrote some of his finest love poetry, born from his own deepest feelings for a person, now lost, and the old haunts—Boscastle, the Valency in spring, and Beeny Cliff:

> *O the opal and the sapphire of that wandering western sea,*
> *And the woman riding high above with bright hair flapping free—*
> *The woman whom I love so, and who loyally loved me.*

It was now more than 40 years since the first visit when he had walked beside Emma as she rode on Beeny Cliff, but to him the memory was clear and the experience more acute for being lost:

> *Still in its chasmal beauty bulks old Beeny to the sky,*
> *And shall she and I not go there once again now March is nigh,*
> *And the sweet things said in that March say anew there by and by?*

The Valency is one of the most beautiful streams in north Cornwall: two miles west is perhaps the most mysterious and dramatic, flowing along Rocky Valley to the sea. We can follow the narrow path beside the stream, which leads past a ruined mill where some mysterious ancient rock carvings are preserved. On goes the stream through the lonely valley until it reaches the sea. No harbour marks the meeting of stream and sea here, no sandy beach lies sheltered by headlands. The water flows over bare rocks, and abruptly falls into the Atlantic which surges restlessly against the black cliffs. The end of Rocky Valley aptly justifies its name. The stream ends in this savage gash in the cliff wall, and the stone glistens dramatically in the sea-spray.

Yet the stream, short though it is, has already had a remarkable life. After its early reaches it arrives at the waterfall at St Nectan's Kieve. We can make the journey here on foot from the coastal road. A lane brings us down into the valley amid thick woods, and the path leads upstream by the water's edge. The further we go, the more mysterious the glen becomes; the vegetation grows more luxuriant and the sides of the gorge rise on either side. Eventually we climb the side of the ravine and gain access to the waterfall.

As we descend the steep path, the roar of the water grows louder and we arrive at the foot of the falls. Through a narrow rent in the rock the stream hurls itself in a cascade 40 feet into a basin, the Kieve, and bursts through a natural arch to plunge into a pool and make for the wooded undergrowth. Few places in the whole of Cornwall are as atmospheric as this; the leap of the water contrasts with the brooding mystery of the glen, overshadowed with dark branches and dank ferns. It is not surprising that it is said to have been the dwelling of hermit and eccentric. It is a place to excite the imagination and haunt the memory.

From Rocky Valley the coastal road climbs up through the old village of Bossiney to its more recent neighbour Tintagel. The chief interest in the village itself is the Old Post Office, owned by the National Trust. Its name refers to its use as a post office in the nineteenth century, but it is in fact a medieval building, a rare survival of a small manor house of the fourteenth century. A low, intimate house with a delightfully crazy slate roof, it has weathered the centuries, and gives the impression of having always been there, part of the natural scene. The rest of the village appears very new by comparison, and is indeed for the most part a Victorian development.

Older than the manor house is the church, though this is not in the village itself. The road winds downhill to cross a stream, taking us past the Elizabethan vicarage and uphill to the church, set boldly facing the sea: even the headstones in the churchyard have buttresses. The church is particularly interesting since with its transepts it is unlike a typical Cornish church. So often in Cornish churches the tower is the only medieval survival with the body of the building reconstructed, but here we can see a good deal of the Norman masonry—indeed a doorway on the north side is probably even older. There is much of interest in the church, including the old screen and an inscribed stone from the Roman period, but the abiding memory is of the setting of the building, bleak and exposed, high above the sea.

It is the sea and coast which have made Tintagel what it is. Dominating the haven is the dramatic headland known as the Island, the centrepiece of Tintagel and the real reason for its fame. The great headland, surrounded by rocks and surf and connected to the mainland by a narrow neck, was always an obvious defensive position, and naturally it became the site of a castle. But older than the castle ruins are the remains of a Celtic monastery which existed here probably in the 6th century. The monks lived their hard and primitive lives in small huts, built of stone and turf walls with earthen floors. From this community they set out on missions to preach to the people in the countryside nearby, or laboured on the land and at their studies and prayers.

Centuries passed before the Norman builders started work, under the direction of Reginald, Earl of Cornwall, in the middle of the twelfth century: we can see the remains of the great hall and the chapel. Later building took place on the mainland, and a bridge connected these works with the inner ward across the isthmus. Rebuilding took place at times but eventually the defences were allowed to decay: Leland noted the ruins on his visit in the early sixteenth century. The actual building still surviving is comparatively slight, but wonderfully impressive because of the setting, poised high on the dark cliffs above the restless sea.

The legend of King Arthur broods over the whole of Tintagel; it is in fact its *raison d'être*. The historical Arthur was certainly not a figure to be associated with medieval moated and turreted castles, but a British war-leader who resisted the Saxons in the 5th century. His European fame goes back to Geoffrey of Monmouth, whose wonderful *History of the Kings of Britain* spread the legend far and wide around the whole of the Continent. In England alone it inspired Malory and Spenser and in the Victorian age Tennyson, Matthew Arnold (himself Cornish on his mother's side), Swinburne and Hardy. So began Tintagel's tourist boom, especially

after the railway reached this part of Cornwall; the massive hotel
was built overlooking the Island, and the village adapted itself to
accommodate the visitors.

Other parts of the country have their Arthurian associations,
but nowhere are they so insistent as in Cornwall, and notably in
this part of the county. Not far from Tintagel is Slaughterbridge,
north of Camelford, where Arthur's last battle was fought, while a
few miles to the east is his reputed burial place at Warbstow
Bury. Bodmin Moor preserves the names of King Arthur's Hall
and King Arthur's Bed, and tradition associates Dozmary Pool
with Excalibur and claims Castle-an-Dinas as the King's hunting
lodge. Cold reason may find little solid connection between
Arthur and Tintagel. Yet at the Island, with the echo of the
Atlantic in Merlin's Cave at its foot, the spirit of the past is all-
powerful and one is prepared to hear the note that Swinburne
caught in his 'Autumn in Cornwall':

> *Full-charged with oldworld wonders,*
> *From dusk Tintagel thunders*
> *A note that smites and sunders*
> *   The hard frore fields of air;*
> *A trumpet stormier-sounded*
> *That once from lists rebounded*
> *When strong men sense-confounded*
> *   Fell thick in tourney there.*

Legend associated the spirit of Arthur with the Cornish chough.
This handsome bird with its red legs and bill was once to be seen
on this coast, but its numbers declined in the last century and it
has now forsaken the area. Another bird whose numbers have
decreased over the last two decades, largely due to the use of pes-
ticides, is the peregrine. However, these cliffs are still a breeding
ground of these magnificent predators, notable for the sheer speed
and power of their stoop, like that of an eagle. The kestrel and
sparrow-hawk are also plentiful in the county, while buzzards are
often to be seen soaring over the valleys. The fortunate observer
may see a harrier, and in the lonelier districts one may hear the
croak of a raven or see it somersault in flight.

The Cornish coasts offer opportunities for watching many varieties of sea-birds, in addition to the inevitable clamorous gulls. A
few colonies of kittiwakes exist, while cormorants and shags are
abundant. Numbers of razorbills are increasing, though guillemots seem to be declining in numbers and sadly the puffin popu-

lation is now small. One of the most spectacular sights occurs in autumn when processions of birds can be seen as their migration routes bring them close to north coast headlands, particularly the Island at St Ives. Guillemots, razorbills, skuas and shearwaters are among the species to be seen, together with gannets with their wonderful six-foot wing-span.

From the coast south of Tintagel, with its views to Rumps Point guarding the entrance to the Camel estuary, we come to Trebarwith Strand and Tregardock Beach, where low tide exposes fine stretches of sand. At one time slate was exported here, for this is one of the principal slate-quarrying areas in Cornwall. It is possible that the great quarry at Delabole was worked in Roman times. It has certainly seen four centuries of continuous work, and is now a vast excavation of about a quarter of a mile across and about 400 feet deep. The beautiful blue slate is used not only for roofing purposes, but for building as well; many houses in the area show the versatility of the material. Besides headstones in churchyards, slate memorials are an important feature of many Cornish churches, particularly in the north and east of the county; this unique craft was at its height in the Elizabethan age and the early seventeenth century, and the standard of carving was often remarkably high.

The railway which formerly served this part of Cornwall ran close to the quarry at Delabole. Its journey north took it alongside the upper waters of the River Camel, and it then turned east to find the valley of the Kensey on its way to Launceston. In the upper reaches of the Inny, running parallel to the Kensey, is the hamlet of St Clether, with its church set on the slope above the river. More important than the church, however, is the holy well half a mile over the fields beside the river.

Cornwall has innumerable holy wells, many of them of great antiquity. In the age of the Celtic saints natural springs were regarded with reverence, and often became associated with a sacred site. Centuries afterwards, in later medieval times, when the churches were being rebuilt and enlarged, several of the holy wells had the added dignity of a stone structure built over them. Here at St Clether, below overhanging rocks in the solitude of the Inny valley, is one of the finest examples; it was restored at the end of the last century by Baring-Gould, famous as hymn-writer and novelist. The well itself has a steep little canopy over it, and from here the water, making for the Inny, flows through a chapel com-

plete with ancient altar stone. It is well worth the walk to visit this
quiet shrine, which preserves something of the solitary spirit of
Celtic Christianity.

Another holy well is preserved two miles away at Laneast, an
attractive village on the hill above a luxuriant part of the Inny. A
Norman church stood here, rebuilt as usual in the fourteenth and
fifteenth centuries, and much old work remains from this time in
wagon roofs, screen, bench-ends and glass. A memorial commemorates Cornwall's most famous astronomer, who was born
here—John Couch Adams, the discoverer of the planet Neptune.
He became Professor of Astronomy at Cambridge in 1858, but his
discovery was the result of work he undertook soon after taking
his degree in 1843. The purpose of this was to find out the reason
for irregularities noticed in the motion of the planet Uranus. In
fact he was not alone in working on this problem: Leverrier reached
identical conclusions at the same time, and in 1848 the Astronom-
ical Society awarded honours equally to both men.

Flowing roughly parallel to the Inny, and joining it just below
Polyphant, is the stream known as Penpont Water. The only village on this stream is Altarnun, lying close to the hamlet of Five
Lanes on the A30 between Launceston and Bodmin. The village
street winds down the hill to the stream, crossed by a modern
bridge and an older pack-horse bridge which leads to the churchyard gate. The church stands at the northern end of the village,
a remarkably fine building, sometimes described as 'the Cathedral
of the Moor': moorland comprises much of the parish, which is in
extent the largest in the whole county.

The tower, of moorland granite, is a noble structure, one of the
tallest in Cornwall. On entering the building one's eye is caught
by the Norman font, large and boldly carved with arresting faces
at each corner. There is certainly the air of a cathedral about the
spacious interior with its barrel roofs. A screen runs across the
width of the three aisles, and beyond it there is a similar spread of
the late seventeenth-century communion rails. The glory of the
church, however, is the set of bench-ends, one of the finest in
Cornwall and the work of a craftsman who has left his name for
us—Robert Daye, who produced the set over a period of years in
the early sixteenth century. The usual symbols of the Passion are
represented, along with Renaissance designs, and there are local
touches with greater individuality such as grazing sheep, musicians and a jester.

In the churchyard is the tomb of Digory Isbell and his wife Elizabeth. These worthy folk lived at nearby Trewint, and in 1743 gave hospitality to John Wesley and his party on their first visit to Cornwall. The friendly welcome the Wesleys regularly found here was by no means their invariable reception in the county. An effigy of the founder of Methodism can be seen over the door of the Wesleyan chapel in Altarnun.

This effigy is an example of the work of a local man, Nevill Northey Burnard, who was born here in 1818. His father was a mason, and the boy followed the family trade, but his talent was out of the ordinary. His work was noticed, and eventually gained him and introduction to Chantrey. Expert guidance made him one of the most successful sculptors in the country, exhibiting at the Royal Academy. Sadly, however, his later years saw a decline in his fortunes. Drink took its toll, his friends deserted him, work ceased. He left London, returning to Cornwall to tramp the roads, until his death in 1878 on a winter's day in the workhouse at Redruth—a sad end for one who had set out with so bright a prospect from the moorland village beside Penpont Water.

From Five Lanes the main road climbs to Trewint, where the charming simplicity of the Isbells' house remains as a reminder of the visits of the Methodists, and then strikes boldly south-west across the Moor towards Bodmin. This is now a trunk road carrying streams of traffic, particularly in the summer, and is being improved so that vehicles can hurtle at even greater speeds across the great open spaces. How different things were before the first turnpike road made the journey across the Moor a comparatively easy matter.

It was in 1769 that provision was first made for a road linking Launceston with Bodmin, the old county town with its eventual successor. The early Methodists were among those who had to follow a mere track, which it was no difficult matter to lose. The regular roads—and these were themselves fairly primitive—skirted the Moor to north and south. The main road still has no links to the north after Five Lanes for seven or eight miles, though several narrow routes lead south to the old coaching road between Liskeard and Bodmin.

Yet the main road, for all its continual activity, has not destroyed the remoteness of the Moor. It is still possible to recapture the isolation and the mystery, to feel the continuity with the past. We can follow the turnpike road through Temple, since the modern route now takes a northerly detour to avoid the village, and cross the stream by the eighteenth-century bridge. It often needs only a short walk to leave behind the obvious signs of the twentieth century, to see the open downs rolling away to distant tors, much as in medieval times and for centuries before.

The basis of the Moor is granite. It is the easternmost and largest of the four main granite areas of the country, part of a chain extending westwards from Dartmoor to the Isles of Scilly. Like the other areas it is surrounded by its metamorphic aureole; this is the region of contact between granite and the surrounding 'killas' (as these slates and shales are known in Cornwall), rich in mineral ores by no means yet exhausted. The mineral extractive industries are not the only activities competing for the use of the Moor; china clay working is all too obvious, granite is quarried particularly on the west side of the Moor; space is required for reservoirs, for afforestation, for more intensive farming.

By comparison with Dartmoor or the moorland areas of the north, Bodmin Moor is not on a grand scale; it is about ten miles in each direction. Nor is it a region of great heights: Brown Willy reaches 1375 feet and Roughtor 1311. Yet these hills are among the oldest in the country. Different approaches produce endless variety in their aspect, and it is not always the highest which are the most arresting; from the south-east the eye is caught by the cone of Sharp Tor, not a lofty hill but dominating the landscape with its bold outline.

The highest hills are on the northern side of the Moor. *Bron ewhella* (the highest hill), or in its corrupted form Brown Willy, and its jagged neighbour Roughtor form the twin peaks of the granite massif. Roughtor is protected by the National Trust, and is easily accessible thanks to the road from Camelford; a medieval chapel of St Michael once crowned its summit, which now carries a memorial to men of the 43rd (Wessex) Division. The two northern hills are visible for miles in many directions, even from the far west of the county. The other dramatic sequence is on the eastern flank of the Moor, where Hawk's Tor, Trewortha Tor and Kilmar Tor stand guard above the upper reaches of the Lynher. This is the area known as Twelve Men's Moor, the twelve men in question holding the land from the Priory of Launceston; this was in the thirteenth century, yet seven centuries are but little in the history of the Moor and the men who have left their mark upon it.

Among the oldest remains of early occupation is the henge

known as the Stripple Stones on the west side of the Moor. Perhaps 4,000 years have elapsed since the circular ditch and bank were constructed. Since the bank is outside the ditch, this site was presumably for ritual purposes rather than as a fortification, but several fortified sites exist on the Moor. One is on the obviously defensible summit of Roughtor, another on the shoulder of Bray Down in the north-east, and several can be found on the south and east of the Moor. Stone circles occur in many parts, notably in the neighbourhood of the earthwork known as King Arthur's Hall. This area and the south-east fringe of the Moor are thick with ancient monuments, often not so far from industrial activity of the present or the recent past. For example the china clay works at Stannon overlook the hut settlements on the slopes of Roughtor.

More recent is the little hamlet of Temple, formerly on the road across the Moor, but now lying quietly away from the main route. Its little church nestles under the slope of the hill, a late Victorian building. Its medieval predecessor was part of a hospice established here in the twelfth century by the Knights Templar for the benefit of travellers across the Moor. Its isolation seems to have contributed to its later notoriety, such as the occasion when sheep-stealing resulted in the hanging of the entire male population—both of them. After the Reformation Temple came under Crown jurisdiction, outside the control of the bishop, and until 1774 acted rather as a Cornish Gretna Green: despite the decay of the church building, several illicit marriages took place here.

Still more recent is the hamlet of Bolventor, situated at the junction of two of the roads from the south with the main highway across the Moor. It has its own church, built in the mid-nineteenth century, but the principal attraction of this hilltop settlement is the slate-hung Jamaica Inn. In coaching days the Inn was a staging post for changing horses; nowadays it does a busy trade particularly in the summer, its popularity increased since it became the title of a well-known historical novel.

Bodmin Moor has a variety of rugged tors and infant rivers, hut settlements, barrows and stone circles, but one feature is unique: the mysterious inland lake known as Dozmary Pool, near the road leading south from Bolventor to St Neot. A brooding atmosphere seems to linger here, and it is not surprising that legends have become associated with the quiet lake, perhaps a mile in circumference. Although it has no significant depth—one can wade across it—Dozmary was long thought to be bottomless and became identified as the scene of the return of Excalibur in the Arthurian saga. Curiously persistent was the association with the legend of Tregeagle, a piece of folk lore linked with an historical figure of the seventeenth century.

Jan Tregeagle was steward of the Robartes family at Lanhydrock, between Bodmin and Lostwithiel, a rapacious and unjust man, but powerful enough to keep his position secure, and at his death he was buried with ceremony at St Breock, near Wadebridge. However, his misdeeds were revealed when his spirit was dramatically summoned to appear as a witness in a court case. To expiate his evildoing he was set to work emptying Dozmary Pool with a perforated limpet shell. One night amid the howling of a storm he fled to sanctuary at Roche Rock, pursued by devils. No rest could he find, and he toiled at the endless task of plaiting ropes of sand.

Dozmary Pool is one of the most ancient sites in Cornwall, for there is evidence of the manufacture of flints here in Mesolithic times. But it is easy to forget reality here in this lonely place, particularly in a fading light, with the sombre mass of Brown Gelly in the distance and a chill wind raising shivers on the face of the water. It is not so easy then to deny the hand brandishing the great sword, or the demons gathering to torment the lonely figure with the limpet shell.

THREE

The Southern Moor
and the Looe Rivers

Bodmin Moor once followed the example of Dartmoor and Exmoor, which take their names from the principal rivers flowing from them. Fowey Moor seems a more attractive name than Bodmin Moor, and is certainly more appropriate. The source of the Fowey is in the solitude of High Moor, a mile to the east of Brown Willy.

There are three distinct stages to the life of the river of its journey of 36 miles to the sea. The youthful stream runs freely in its south-easterly course across the open moor, attended by a road as far as Draynes Bridge. Here a change takes place. The stream is now a mature river, and as it turns away towards the west so it flows through wooded country, indeed through some of the most picturesque inland scenery in the county, until it arrives at the tidal reach at Lostwithiel. Now the third phase in the river's life begins; the pace slows, and the water makes its leisurely way south to the broad estuary and out to the open sea of the English Channel.

Not far below Draynes Bridge where the wooded stretch begins the river tumbles over the rocks at picturesque Golitha Falls, the haunt of dipper and wagtail. A couple of miles further downstream the river is spanned by the medieval Treverbyn Bridge. Fortunately a new bridge has been built alongside the ancient structure, which has thus been preserved, escaping the fate of many old bridges which have been widened and as a result have lost their character. This bridge, dating from 1412, was formerly of greater importance, when the main road from Liskeard to Bodmin followed this route to St Neot, avoiding the marshy ground of the Glynn valley. Since the early nineteenth century the main road has taken traffic through the valley, scenically a rewarding route though sometimes frustrating to the driver intent only on speed. The valley has further significance for communications since the main railway line between Liskeard and Lostwithiel follows this route, no mean feat of engineering.

Let us retrace our steps to the upper reaches of the river and the fresh moorland which gives it birth. Various aspects of Cornwall have their devotees: the dramatic coast confronting the wild Atlantic; the attractive fishing villages; graceful curving beaches; wind-swept tors of the high moors; wooded slopes rising from the water's edge along tidal estuaries. Each of these has its particular beauty, and has its praises sung regularly. But some of the most beautiful parishes in Cornwall are those on the edge of the Moor, which have a beauty of their own; perhaps a more subtle beauty, but for all that a characteristic part of the Cornish scene. To the south of the Moor lie Cardinham, Warleggan, St Neot, whose rivers flow to join the Fowey, and east of St Cleer the parishes on the Lynher, Linkinhorne and North Hill. In Bronze Age times, the most populous parts of Cornwall were the high areas of the moors, but a changing climate led men to forsake the harsh uplands which were now unsuitable for agriculture. Yet the valleys, with their marshes and forests, were equally uninviting, and so the land on the edges of the moor became desirable for development; consequently these areas have the longest history of settlement, from that remote era to our own time.

At North Hill the Withey Brook finishes its lonely journey from Stowe's Hill, skirting Twelve Men's Moor and King Arthur's Bed and running down through steep wooded country to the Lynher. Stone from quarries here was shipped to London and used in the building of Westminster Bridge. The church is ambitious, the interior dignified and with several interesting features. Both nave and aisles have fine wagon roofs, and here is one of the finest of seventeenth-century Cornish monuments, commemorating members of the Spoure family; their painted effigies stand or kneel opposite each other with engaging simplicity and naivety.

Following the Lynher downstream we come to the parish of Linkinhorne, an excellent example of the Cornish characteristic of small hamlets rather than one central village. The churchtown itself contains a small proportion of the population, which is spread around such neighbouring settlements as Rilla Mill, Upton

Cross and Minions. The church at Linkinhorne traditionally owes much to the same Henry Trecarrel of Lezant whose generosity enriched the church at Launceston. In particular he is credited with the building of the tower, a fourstage giant second only to Probus in height.

From the fertile country of the Lynher valley the road climbs westward to the parish of St Cleer, and here is a remarkable contrast, for we are on the edge of the Moor and among many reminders of the past. This was formerly a thriving mining area, as the ruined engine-houses remind us, and also a centre for granite quarrying. North of Minions is the quarry at Stowe's Hill, where the hillside has been eaten away gradually as the granite has been hewn out. The dramatic effect of the quarry is heightened by the natural landscape, for crowning Stowe's Hill is the famous rock formation known as the Cheesewring, an immense pile of weather-worn boulders; the large slabs appear to be so precariously perched that a collapse is imminent, yet they have stood silently here for countless centuries before men first came to gaze at them in awe. Now the rocks are perched on the edge of the quarry, and from the hill a breathtaking view can be seen: both coasts are visible; to the south-east rises the mine-scarred Caradon Hill, now crowned with its twentieth-century adornment—a television mast; away to the east beyond the shoulder of Kit Hill are outlined the heights of Dartmoor, while to the north and west the mysterious moorland carries the eye to the distant tors.

Primitive men have left several relics of their presence in this area. South of the Cheesewring are the three stone circles known as the Hurlers. The original purpose of the circles is not clear, though presumably they served some ceremonial function, but the name was attached much later when they were brought into service as a warning against Sabbath-breakers, the two menhirs ('longstones') standing nearby playing the part of the Pipers who provided music for the sacrilegious game. Between the mining hamlet of Darite and St Cleer is another Neolithic survival, and this one of the finest examples of its kind in Cornwall: Trethevy Quoit. This is the remains of a burial chamber, consisting of vertical slabs of granite surmounted by a massive capstone. Originally enclosed in earth, centuries of weathering have laid the megaliths bare, and it appears now as it did in 1584 when John Norden in his *Topographical Description of Cornwall* wrote of it as 'a little house raised of mighty stones, standing on a little hill within a field'.'

Of a later century, though still remote from our time, is King Doniert's Stone, thought to commemorate a 9th-century king of Cornwall who was drowned in the nearby River Fowey. The stone stands beside the road between Redgate and Common Moor, and is inscribed 'DONIERT ROGAVIT PRO ANIMA'. St Cleer village was formerly the centre of this mining area, at one time a small town of 4,000 people. Like Linkinhorne, St Cleer possesses a holy well, this one being among the finest in the county; it has been protected since the fifteenth century by a granite building with pillars, rounded arches and a steeply-pitched roof.

Although the sea is never far away, and innumerable streams run from the moors either directly to the sea or into the larger rivers. Cornwall can claim only two natural lakes of any size. On the other hand, within recent years, as greater demands have been made on the water supply, so reservoirs have been created to satisfy these needs. In the far west is Drift Reservoir, near Sancreed; inland from Newquay is Porth Reservoir, in the parish of Colan; Crowdy Reservoir lies on the northern edge of Bodmin Moor. Between Camborne and Falmouth are Argal Reservoir and its larger neighbour at Stithians, while here on the southern flank of Bodmin Moor just north of St Cleer is the comparatively new Siblyback Reservoir.

Few projects seem to generate such passionate debate as the siting of reservoirs. Not only the urban landscape but also much of the countryside owes its appearance to man's activities over the centuries, and his record is not always praiseworthy, particularly since the Industrial Revolution. Cornwall has its share of scars. But it is difficult to regard these lakes, however artificial may be their origin, as other than an enhancement of the landscape. The sickle-shaped Siblyback is an excellent example; sensible planting adds to the charm of the lake's situation, and as a recreational centre it attracts fishermen and yachtsmen, so its benefits are by no means limited to the primary object of conserving water.

We now rejoin the River Fowey where it begins the wooded stage of its journey at Draynes Bridge, and here we enter the parish of St Neot. An extensive parish it is, the second largest in Cornwall, including a sizeable area of Bodmin Moor, but with a recognizable centre at the attractive village of St Neot itself. Here an eighteenth-century bridge crosses the St Neot River—or Loveny, to restore its charming old name—which drains the moorland north of the village (including a stream from Dozmary Pool), and flows through its own wooded valley to join the Fowey at Two Waters Foot.

Yet another holy well is preserved here, near the river to the north of the village. Here, according to tradition, the saint immersed himself in water up to the neck during his daily recitation of the psalter. The parish is rich in ancient crosses, the finest being in the churchyard, just beside the church door. This is undoubtedly one of the best granite crosses in the county, with Celtic designs carved on each of the four sides of the shaft.

The church itself dominates the village, from whichever direction we approach, and is the pride of its people now as much as in the fifteenth and sixteenth centuries when it was so much enriched. Built against a hillside as it is, the main decorative work of the exterior is concentrated on the south side, and here we see an embattled south aisle, incorporating a two-storeyed porch with a fine stone vaulting. Impressive though the building itself is, it contains a further glory which has made it famous throughout Cornwall and beyond—its stained glass.

The splendid sequence of windows represents the devotion of the pre-Reformation villagers towards their church. Some reflect the generosity of individual families whose names they preserve, other were donated by representative groups, such as the Wives' Window and the Young Women's Window. Not all the glass is original; a major restoration was undertaken by John Hedgeland in the 1820's, and more work has been necessary in recent years, but a large amount of original glass remains, seen to the best advantage on a sunny day.

Several of the windows represent saints, ranging from Apostles to local Celtic saints, but there are four elaborate series of scenes, the finest of which is the Creation window in the Lady Chapel. This includes the well-known episodes from Genesis, and also a representation of the legend of Seth planting a seed in the mouth of the dead Adam, from which the tree would grow yielding the wood of the true cross. The story of Noah is the theme of another of these windows, and in the opposite corner of the church is a dramatic series of scenes from the life of St George. Finally, near St George in the north aisle is the life of St Neot himself, with illustrations of his pious life and some miraculous events associated with him. Incidentally, the identity of St Neot has caused some confusion: it seems clear now that the Saxon St Neot associated with King Alfred has no connection with Cornwall, and that the former name of St Anietus preserves the true identity of the Celtic saint to whom the church is dedicated.

The old coaching road from Liskeard to Bodmin now comes to the picturesque Pantersbridge. Just above this bridge the River Bedalder is joined by the Dewy, and, like the Loveny, these streams drain this part of the Moor and flow south to join the Fowey. The Bedalder is often known as the Warleggan River, from the parish through which it flows, mostly taking in moorland territory, the main settlement being at Mount, on the old coach route. The churchtown stands up above the wooded gorge of the river, with its low two-aisled church secluded among trees; it never seems to have recovered from the day in 1818 when lightning struck the tower, and the spire was destroyed. The eccentricity of the last independent rector only increased the uneasy atmosphere which seems to brood over this lonely place; to the south are the woods, the river and the busy highway, but always over one's shoulder is the silence of the Moor.

To the west of Warleggan is the parish of Cardinham, geographically similar to its neighbour, with a river running down to join the Fowey. Like St Neot, the parish possesses several crosses, including one of the county's finest examples, large and elaborately carved, in the churchyard. The church itself is a large building for the area it serves, and is worth seeing for its modern glass, and, of earlier days, a fine set of bench-ends and a very early fifteenth-century brass.

The Cardinham river joins the Fowey near Bodmin Road Station, where the road and railway branch line to the county town turn north away from the valley, and here is the square porticoed Regency house of Glynn. Major-General Sir Richard Hussey Vivian, Baron Vivian of Glynn and Truro, a Peninsular War veteran, played a major part as a cavalry commander in the Waterloo campaign; Cornishmen indeed aver that the victory was due to his efforts. It was to this stately house that he retired, to live with his memories amidst the beauty of the wooded valley of the Fowey.

The regional capital for the south-east side of the Moor is Liskeard. The site of a Domesday manor, the town followed the typical pattern of becoming a borough in the thirteenth century, with the establishment of a market and fair. Lying at the head of the valley of the Looe River, which, like the neighbouring West Looe River, rises in the parish, it occupies a significant position on the southern route into the county. A coastal route from the Cremyll ferry made use of ferries and the bridge at Looe, but the routes from the Saltash ferry and from New Bridge at Gunnislake converged at Liskeard, avoiding the south coast valleys and making for Lostwithiel. Eventually the railway followed the same route from Saltash, and since the opening of the new Tamar Bridge, road traffic on this route has increased dramatically. Liskeard used to be one of the worst bottlenecks in Cornwall, but the recently constructed by-pass has ensured that the bulk of traffic between Plymouth and west Cornwall does not have to pass through the town, and has thereby restored some of its peace.

For Liskeard is a town of pleasant character. As the mineral resources of the area were developed, so the prosperity of the town increased, and consequently, like Truro further west, Georgian buildings are predominant, centred on the Parade. Attractive terraces of Georgian and early Victorian residences are a feature of the town, but the casual visitor passing through is apt to miss the older part with its slate-hung houses set in the valley between the two hills. The spacious church, standing high on the eastern side of the town, is a mainly fifteenth-century building with a modern tower, second in size only to Bodmin.

The valley of the Looe River provided a natural route to the coast when the developing mines and quarries of the district needed an outlet, and so in 1825 work began on the construction of a canal from Looe to Moorswater, in the valley below the town, a valley now spanned by one of the fine viaducts on the main railway line. For a short time the canal prospered, but it was late in the canal era, and it was not long before it was converted into a single-line branch railway, linked with the main line station at Liskeard in a dramatic curved incline.

The Liskeard and Caradon Railway laid a track from Moorswater to South Caradon, with a later extension to the Cheesewring, and so the connection with the port was established. As with some of the other mineral lines, horse power brought the wagons up the lines, and the full consignments travelled down by gravity. The system north of Liskeard was purely for industrial purposes, not officially carrying passengers (apart from the occasional Sunday School outing), and in 1916 with the decline in the industry this part of the line was closed.

The country around the West Looe River is wonderfully remote, heavily wooded around the course of the river, the lanes full of corners and precipitous hills. Three of these hills converge on Herodsfoot, an attractive village with slate cottages, formerly a lead-mining area, while to the north St Pinnock stands on a hill looking across the valley to Trevelmond on the opposite slope. The finest building in the parish of St Pinnock is the viaduct in the Glynn valley; standing 150 feet high, this is the highest of all the viaducts on this section of the main line.

Following the Looe River south from Liskeard we come first to St Keyne. What has spread the fame of the village and its saint is the holy well by the road down towards the river. Richard Carew related the legend of the well and the properties of its water: it had a powerful influence over a marriage, for whichever partner, husband or wife, drank first from the well would gain the mastery. The story was amplified in ballad form by Robert Southey. He tells how a stranger drank from the well, and then heard about its unusual character from a local countryman who admitted that at his wedding he had left his wife at the church porch in order to hurry to drink at the well, and returned only to find that his quick-witted bride had thought a step ahead of him and taken a bottle to church.

At this point, road and valley wind their way hand in hand down the valley, past the stations familiar and exciting to those who come this way on holiday—Causeland, Sandplace, Looe: the names seem in a way evocative of a sunny afternoon. Close to Sandplace is Morval House, with its attendant church, the house being essentially an Elizabethan building.

The East and West Looe Rivers flow south through their steeply wooded valleys and broaden out into estuaries before joining: Looe derives its name from a Celtic word similar to the Scottish 'loch'. The joint rivers then flow along to the sea through a narrow channel, creating a sheltered harbour which has been the centre of the town's activity for centuries. The river valleys are dramatically beautiful, and would be finer still if Trenant Wood on the promontory between the rivers had not been shaved.

The river flowing through the centre of Looe has effectively divided it into two separate towns, and this has always been the case; indeed, until 1832 East and West Looe each returned two members to Parliament, though by that time the electorate was reduced to a mere handful. The present bridge joining the two communities dates from the middle of the nineteenth century, being widened a century later. It is a pity that the medieval bridge nearer the sea was not preserved when the new bridge was constructed, since contemporary descriptions and drawings suggest that it was almost as fine as those at Wadebridge and Bideford. In fact Looe bridge was the oldest of these long bridges, dating from the early fifteenth century. Indulgences were issued to raise funds for its construction, being a necessary link on the route from Plymouth to Fowey, and it was unique in Cornwall in having a chapel in the middle, dedicated to St Anne. The chapel did not survive the Reformation, but the bridge itself existed until 1853.

Fishing has naturally been an important activity at Looe, but in the fourteenth century the port provided ships and men for use chiefly against the French in the Hundred Years' War. These were turbulent times in a seaport, but this phase of Looe's activity declined and it concentrated on trading and fishing. The Napoleonic War with its trade blockade reduced the town's fortunes, though these revived as the nineteenth century gathered momentum. As we have seen, the railway succeeded the canal from Liskeard in 1860, and this followed the usual pattern of starting with goods traffic and, from 1879, running a passenger service with the rise of tourism.

Now it is the tourist trade on which the town thrives, and for the visitor it is an attractive place, with its beaches and cliff walks. The activity of the harbour provides a focal point, with fishing expeditions, notably in quest of sharks: each season the big game hunters are photographed with their awesome catches. The town preserves its buildings well, with attractive tubs of flowers in the little courts and alleys near the sea front. From the front the narrow streets wind back by the quay with gift shops and cafés to satisfy the visitor, and terraces of houses climb the hills on either side of the harbour where the boats are moored and the gulls endlessly wheel and cry.

The parish church of East Looe is St Martin's by Looe, which shelters by an inland hill with its rectory standing amid beeches. The mother church of West Looe lies two miles to the west at Talland, by a steep hill leading down to Talland Bay, seen to advantage from the churchyard. Externally the most remarkable feature of the church is the tower which seems to grow out of the hillside and is joined to the church by a porch with a wagon-roof. Inside are sixteenth-century bench-ends and some of the best examples of Cornish slate memorials. Talland is also the parish church of Polperro, a mile or so round the corner in the next inlet, which for its size must be one of the best known and most photographed villages in Cornwall.

A stream winds down a steep valley to the sea, and at its mouth developed the usual little harbour of the type which used to grow up at every opportunity in inlets in the cliff wall. The village made its living by fishing, with a certain amount of trading and no small amount of smuggling in former times. Hemmed in by steep hills on both sides, the life of the village centred entirely on the harbour, and the houses cling to the slopes above the water. Later development had to follow the course of the stream up the valley, so that now the village straggles back up the new road which was built to replace the former steep approaches up almost perpendicular hills.

A villager of previous centuries would be hard put to recognize the change in modern Polperro: the same harbour and narrow streets, but now smartened and idealized as a tourist attraction par excellence. And attractive it undoubtedly is, with the little stream bustling along its narrow course between the houses, small picturesque cottages set at all angles and levels along the lanes and alleys. The cliffs on either side of the inlet are protected by the National Trust, and the charm of the little port is irresistible. A touch of imagination as one sits by the harbour mouth can remove the modern veneer, and there is the remote centuries-old settlement of grey cottages tucked under the protective hills, the restless clamour of the gulls and the fishermen wresting their living from this same Cornish sea.

A man who knew and loved Polperro for most of his 81 years was Jonathan Couch. A native of the village, he completed his medical training in London after studying locally and returned to Polperro at the age of 20, devoting the rest of his life to the community as its doctor and general adviser. A sincere Methodist, he cared conscientiously for the welfare of the fishermen and of the industry on which their livelihood depended. Though he rarely left the village, he earned a reputation as an antiquary—publishing a history of Polperro in 1871—but even more so as a naturalist.

Couch was a Cornish Gilbert White, or perhaps a modern Pliny the Elder (whose works, incidentally, he translated and studied). He took full advantage of living in a fishing village, and his own greatest work was his *History of the Fishes of the British Isles,* which appeared in four volumes between 1860 and 1865. He arranged with the fishermen that they would bring anything unusual in their catch for his inspection, and spent hours on detailed drawings of specimens, reproducing their vivid colouring before it faded. He contributed articles on various subjects to journals and magazines, and his fame spread abroad, but here in this remote village he chose to live his eminently useful life: scholar, philanthropist and very much the local 'character'.

Between the West Looe River and the estuary of the Fowey lies a stretch of beautiful country, largely unspoilt. One main road takes traffic to Looe and Polperro, but otherwise the roads are not designed for speed; narrow and winding, they take the traveller over hills and down to wooded valleys, with continually changing views round unexpected corners. Here in this remote country one can really feel lost.

On the main road, a few miles from Polperro, is the village of Pelynt. The church is dedicated to St Nonna, whose holy well stands away down in the steep valley of the West Looe; the nineteenth-century restorer dealt rather harshly with the church, but there is a fine seventeenth-century Tuscan arcade of granite. A pastoral staff and chair are a reminder of the leading family of the parish, since they belonged to Jonathan Trelawny, whose name has become known to generations of Cornishmen—and Englishmen as well.

A staunch supporter of the Stuarts, Trelawny played an active role in suppressing the rebellion of the Duke of Monmouth in 1685, as a result of which the Bishopric of Bristol came his way. The crisis of his life came three years later when James II commanded the clergy to read the Declaration of Indulgence to their congregations. Trelawny and five other bishops supported the Archbishop of Canterbury in resisting the King's wishes, petitioning him to withdraw the order, which was designed to give toleration to Catholics. The bishops were prosecuted for 'publishing a seditious libel', and imprisoned in the Tower. Popular feeling ran high, and the acquittal of the bishops produced a tremendously enthusiastic reaction.

In the last decade of the eighteenth century the family produced another remarkable figure, Edward John Trelawny. Much of his life was spent in travelling, in heroic exploits such as fighting for Greek independence, or in writing of his activities: his *Adventures of a Younger Son* appeared in 1831, and later in his long life he produced volumes of reminiscences of his dealings with Shelley and

Byron. One of the most striking events of his career occurred in 1822, when he was in Italy with Byron, Leigh Hunt and Shelley. After the ill-fated voyage of the *Don Juan* had resulted in the drowning of Shelley, Trelawny organized his cremation on the beach in order that his ashes might be interred at Rome in the Protestant cemetery, an event which he described with vivid and dramatic detail. Nearly 60 years later his last wish was fulfilled when his own remains were laid by the grave of Shelley, in the same cemetery where John Keats was buried.

For Cornishmen this Protestant cemetery at Rome acquired deeper significance in 1933 when it became the last resting place of that beloved Cornish antiquarian Charles Henderson. From boyhood he had been fascinated by Cornish history, and until his tragically early death at the age of 33 he worked incessantly, investigating documents, gathering material, writing articles and lecturing. For his last ten years he lived at the family home of Penmount just outside Truro, an eighteenth-century house in whose garden he loved to work. An Oxford don for the last five years of his life, his historical interests ranged widely, but his great achievement was his work on Cornwall's past, which he studied not only in libraries and muniment-rooms but also around the lanes and streams of the county he came to know so intimately.

FOUR

Fowey and St Austell

Between Looe and the Fowey can occasionally be seen traces of an Iron Age rampart and ditch, known as the Giant's Hedge, probably originating as a tribal boundary. This is most marked in the parish of Lanreath, which also contains the circular fort of Bury Down. The village of Lanreath lies just off the main road, and is quiet and attractive as a result. Near the church is the fine Jacobean manor house of Court. This was once owned by the Grylls family whose memorial is almost unrivalled as a painted wooden monument of considerable delicacy and elaboration. Indeed woodwork is the most notable feature of this church, the interior dominated by the screen which runs across nave and aisle. Many painted figures survive on the panels of the screen, and Jacobean bench-ends, font cover and chancel stalls also remain, so that the interior is among the most charming of all Cornish churches.

To the north-west of Lanreath lies the large estate of Boconnoc, with perhaps the finest park in Cornwall. The house was built mainly in the eighteenth century by the Pitt family, particularly Lord Camelford, friend of Horace Walpole. The grounds consist partly of formal terraces and gardens, largely the work of the Fortescue family in the nineteenth century, and also the grand landscaped park with its woods of oak and beech. Here is the oldest of Cornish deer-parks, existing for over 500 years and still bordered by its ancient dyke. The drive north-east from the house takes us past the obelisk erected by Lord Camelford in 1771 to his uncle Sir Richard Lyttleton, and through the woods to the gate opposite Braddock church.

The countryside around here breathes a spirit of quiet and

tranquillity, but three centuries ago the rural peace was rudely broken. For this area was one of the principal scenes of action in the county when Cornwall had its part to play in the Civil War. When hostilities began in August 1642 Cornwall generally supported the Royalist cause; beyond the Tamar the western counties of England were principally supporting Parliament, and Plymouth continually held up the Royalist advance. The greater Cornish gentry were for the King, apart from Lord Robartes of Lanhydrock. Ideological differences were not generally the decisive factor for the bulk of the people, whose loyalties lay nearer home; indeed the majority had no choice but were pressed into service.

A force of Royalist militia drove the Parliamentary forces back to their base at Saltash and then beyond the Tamar to Plymouth. Though the force consisted of Cornishmen, their leader was a 'foreigner', Sir Ralph Hopton, an experienced soldier and a fine commander. With the aid of such local Royalist gentry as Sir Bevil Grenville, to whom the Cornishmen could feel some allegiance, Hopton raised and equipped a small volunteer force. A counter-attack began in January 1643. The major force under the Earl of Stamford was preceded by an advance guard under Colonel Ruthven, which did not wait for the main contingent but advanced west from Liskeard and prepared for battle on Braddock Downs. Hopton's army was at nearby Boconnoc, and the battle of 19 January resulted in a convincing victory for the Royalists, who pursued the fugitives to Saltash and out of the county.

The next move was an advance of Parliamentary troops under the Earl of Stamford himself. This force crossed the upper reaches of the Tamar and advanced into north Cornwall, taking up a strong position on a hill on the north side of Stratton. When Hopton's army reached Stratton from Launceston he decided to attack without delay, despite being outnumbered and short of supplies. So next day, 16 May, the Cornishmen repeatedly attacked the hill; the day wore on, and ammunition ran low. Now the order was given to charge, and not to stop to fire until the summit was reached. This courageous action had its reward: the defenders broke and fled. The defeated commander left nothing except his name at the site of the battle—Stamford Hill. Cornwall was firmly in Royalist hands, and the Cornishmen, disciplined and devoted to their leaders, had built up for themselves both self-confidence and reputation.

Cornish forces now played an important part in the Royalist victories at Lansdown and Roundway Down, then at the successful siege of Bristol. The King himself was grateful for the contribution made by the Cornish to his cause, and from his camp at Sudeley Castle in the Cotswolds he sent a message to 'all his loving Subjects in the County of Cornwall'. 'We are highly sensible', he wrote, 'of the extraordinary Merits of our County of Cornwall; of their Zeal for the Defence of our Person, and the just Rights of our Crown, in a time when we could contribute so little to our own Defence, or their Assistance.' He decreed that a copy of the letter should be set up in every church in the county, and some of these still survive.

Late in July 1644 the King advanced west through Devon, in pursuit of a Parliamentary army under the command of the Earl of Essex, who crossed the Tamar at Horse Bridge and advanced into the centre of the county. Sir Richard Grenville's army lay to the west, while Hopton brought a force to join the King and Prince Maurice at Launceston. As the Royalists advanced, the Parliamentary army was caught in the peninsula between Lostwithiel and Fowey. As August wore on, Essex's position grew more desperate. The night of the 30th was dark and wet, and the cavalry took their chance to elude the besieging forces and make for Saltash and safety. Essex had hoped to lead the infantry to Fowey and embark them thence for Plymouth, but the weather delayed his progress. On the heights at Castle Dore they were besieged by the Royalists. As September dawned, Essex and Robartes quietly left the field and made for Plymouth in a small boat. The remainder of the army surrendered, and embarked on a terrible march back to the Tamar: only a small proportion returned safely to Dorset. The King was able to leave Cornwall firmly under Royalist control.

However, the outcome of the war was now being determined by the creation of the New Model Army under Fairfax and Cromwell. As summer succeeded spring 1645 Fairfax led his army relentlessly westwards, and throughout the summer months the Royalist strongholds capitulated. In the early months of 1646 the Royalists were compelled to retreat, and Prince Charles, the nominal commander of the western army, left Pendennis for the Isles of Scilly, under the care of Edward Hyde, Earl of Clarendon, who was later to write the history of the Great Rebellion.

Hopton, perhaps reflecting on the changed fortunes since the victories of three years earlier, was forced to retreat as far as Truro. On 10 March peace terms were discussed at Tresillian Bridge, and two days later Hopton signed the instrument of surrender. After a month St Michael's Mount capitulated, as the Prince and his Council left the Isles of Scilly for Jersey and the Continent. Gallant old Sir John Arundell refused to surrender Pendennis Castle until driven by extremes of starvation: the final act of the war in Cornwall came on 17 August, when the garrison finally marched out, determined to the last.

The Giant's Hedge ends at Lerryn, a pretty village at the tidal head of the creek, the longest tributary of the Fowey estuary. The east side of the upper estuary contains the parishes of St Winnow and St Veep, beautiful remote country with a complete contrast in the situation of the two churches. St Veep stands on a hill, low and solid for protection against the winds; St Winnow occupies one of the most beautiful settings of any church in Cornwall, down beside the river, looking across to the woods of Lantyan. There is an array of bench-ends, including a medieval cog, or cargo-boat, and a peasant drinking from a leather bottle, a beautiful rood screen and a complete window of medieval glass showing saints and the donors with their heraldic arms. The farm buildings and vicarage make a delightful group with the church, and from the churchyard we see the river curving away up to Lostwithiel on the one hand and in the other direction broadening out between the wooded banks and away to the sea.

South of St Veep is another long arm of the estuary, Penpoll Creek, and beyond it again the parish of Lanteglos-by-Fowey. The National Trust owns stretches of the coast at Lantic Bay and further east at Lantivet Bay, where the tower of Lansallos church can be glimpsed from the cliff-top. Also in the care of the Trust is much of the eastern end of the estuary, particularly the shores of the beautiful Pont Pill and the hamlet of Pont itself, where it has done excellent work rebuilding the quay and footbridge. Polruan guards the eastern side of the entrance to Fowey harbour, at one time literally when a chain ran across the harbour mouth restricting access to the port and barring the passage to intruders. The remains of a blockhouse survive as a reminder of those independent days.

A passenger ferry connects Polruan with Fowey, but the vehicle ferry lies higher up the river, crossing from Fowey to the smaller village of Bodinnick. To reach Bodinnick from Polruan we must take the road around the head of Pont Pill, below the churchtown of Lanteglos. Isolated, apart from the neighbouring farm buildings, this exquisite church is sequestered and unspoilt; the churchyard contains a fine lantern cross, and inside are bench-ends, Kempe windows and brasses to the Mohun family who once owned the land here. The Mohun family seat was at Hall, above Bodinnick, where the remains of the chapel still exist as a farm building, a rare example of a medieval chapel like Trecarrel.

It is from the eastern side of the estuary that the port of Fowey is best observed. We can see the terraces climbing the hillside, which has had a significant influence on the growth of the town; the steep slopes did not encourage the development of a nineteenth-century seaside resort. It is certainly not a place to be seen from a motor car; its narrow streets and steep hills call for exploration on foot, a quest rewarded by several charming buildings of the sixteenth and seventeenth centuries.

The church of St Fimbarrus—an Irish saint—is on a large scale, probably the work of foreign builders, owing to the influence of the Duchy of Cornwall. The use of the clerestory here and at Lostwithiel is almost unexampled elsewhere in Cornwall, and the tower is a splendid four-stage specimen of the Somerset type. The other building of note in the town stands close to the church, Place House, home of the Treffry family. Originally a fortified house, its character was altered in keeping with the times when granite bay windows were added in the reign of Henry VII. However, much more sweeping alteration took place in the early nineteenth century when that remarkable member of the family, J. T. Treffry, built on some striking Regency Gothic additions with a rather fantastic tower and a hall of a variety of Cornish granites, all polished.

The sea has dominated the history of Fowey. From ancient times a trade route linked the Camel estuary on the north coast with the River Fowey, and here was the protected deep-water anchorage facing the coast of Brittany. Before the growth of Anglo-French hostility, there was a regular trade with the Continent from the port. By the outbreak of the Hundred Years' War, Fowey had become the major port on the south coast; the Cornish complement of 47 ships assembled here for Edward III's expedition against Calais in 1347 was the largest contribution of any port in the kingdom. Great rivalry existed between ports, and the men of Fowey recognized no superiors. On one notable occasion

Fowey seamen refused to pay the customary respect when passing
Rye and Winchelsea; the boats which set out to punish this insol-
ence were routed by the 'Gallants of Fowey', who consequently
incorporated the arms of all the Cinque Ports into their own.

Not always did the men of Fowey have things their own way. In
1457 the town was subjected to invasion by the French, who sac-
ked the town and were only repulsed from Place House thanks to
the spirited defence led by the lady of the mansion in her husband's absence. To prevent repetition of this disaster, blockhouses
were built on either side of the harbour, and a chain stretched
across the harbour mouth.

Their independent spirit led the men of Fowey into trouble in
the reign of Edward IV. The harrying of French vessels and ports
by Fowey ships was tolerable while a state of war existed, but
could hardly be permitted in a time of peace. The King sent a
messenger to call the aggressive Cornishmen into line; however,
not only was the messenger insulted (and indeed assaulted) but
raids went on as before. Edward took decisive action: Fowey's
ships and stores, together with the harbour chain, were removed
to Dartmouth, and the port's days as a naval base were over.

However, the port of Fowey continued to flourish, particularly
with the growth of the china clay industry, so that the flags of
many nations would be visible fluttering at the mastheads of ships
thronging the harbour. The town has largely retained its Cornish
character, so that it seems right that so eminent a Cornish writer
as Sir Arthur Quiller-Couch should have worked here, in the
'Troy Town' he made so well known. And it is reflected through
other eyes, those of Q's friend Kenneth Grahame, who loved 'the
little grey sea town' and the river, and from his own experience
here wove the magic of *The Wind in the Willows*.

It is now only the seaward end of the estuary which is navigable, though formerly vessels could sail for several miles upstream.
Having left the sea behind, they would pass the village of Golant,
opposite Penpoll Creek, with its church set on the hill overlooking
the river. This church is dedicated to St Sampson, who is said to
have travelled from Wales to Padstow and followed the trade
route south with his companions. After a stay at Golant he continued to Brittany, where he founded the monastery of Dol.
Walking around Golant, with its ancient holy well and its delightful views of the river, one cannot help feeling that there must have
been a strong temptation for the monastic party to stay here.

It is in this area west of the Fowey that the stories of Tristan and Iseult in the Arthurian legend come to life. Here at Castle Dore was the stronghold of King Mark, a hill-top site first occupied nine centuries previously, while his palace was located in the valley just to the north at Lantyan or perhaps the neighbouring village of Castle. The nearby church of Golant also features in the story. It seems likely that the Forest of Morrois is to be equated with Moresk in the parish of St Clement near Truro, and in this formerly very wooded area the fugitive lovers took shelter. This being so, the ferry at Malpas preserves the name of La Mal Pas, where Iseult crossed on her way to Blancheland, perhaps Nansavallan, south-west of Truro. Much of this identification is naturally conjectural, and may be disputed, but the remarkable discovery of the Tristan Stone near Castle Dore must have real significance. This seven foot high stone bears an inscription from the 6th century commemorating 'Drustanus, son of Cunomorus'. Here, it seems, is a witness to an historical Tristan; however much of the legend we care to consider as fact, this seems to be its true location.

The journey upstream takes us past Penquite, home of Charles Peard, 'Garibaldi's Englishman', a staunch supporter and friend of the Italian general, who visited him here in 1864. The height of the tidal reach is now within two miles at the ancient town of Lostwithiel, where the river is spanned by one of the finest old bridges in the county. The present bridge, which is certainly not the first to be built here, probably dates from 1437, when an Indulgence was granted to raise funds for its construction; five pointed arches carry the road across the river, much silted up since the original building.

The main road from Liskeard to St Austell fortunately uses a new bridge to the north of the town, which has not only saved the medieval bridge from the impossible task of coping with modern traffic but has largely preserved the town itself. Lostwithiel grew up at the strategic river crossing, under the eye of neighbouring Restormel Castle, and, in common with the majority of older towns in Cornwall, became a borough during the twelfth century. In the mid-thirteenth century castle and town came under the control of Richard, Earl of Cornwall, a brother of Henry III. At his death in 1272, his son Edward succeeded to the earldom and not only resided at Restormel but fostered the growth and importance of the nearby town. Official buildings appeared, including the Duchy Palace and the Shire Hall, to house the machinery of government.

In 1337 Edward III created the Duchy of Cornwall out of the original Norman earldom to support his eldest son, Edward the Black Prince, who paid his first visit to his Duchy in 1354. Since the founding of the Duchy the eldest son of the sovereign has been born Duke of Cornwall; in the absence of a male heir the title lies dormant in the Crown. To correct a popular misconception, the Duchy of Cornwall is not synonymous with the County of Cornwall; it is in fact a great estate, much (though by no means all) of its lands being in Cornwall, belonging to the sovereign's eldest son. And it was the proximity to Restormel Castle that resulted in Lostwithiel being the centre of Duchy administration.

The main street of Lostwithiel is simply charming in character. The guildhall was given by the Earl of Mount Edgcumbe in the eighteenth century. The sophisticated and elaborate spire of the church is quite un-Cornish; broached, with dormer windows, it is more reminiscent of Brittany or Gascony, with which the Duchy had trading connections. As at Fowey there is the unusual feature of a clerestory, and the splendid fourteenth-century tracery of the east window is among the finest examples of its type in Cornwall. From much the same date is the font; it is carved with a hunting scene depicting a medieval knight, falcon on wrist, and a dog catching a hare, portraying what must have been a familiar sight in the great park surrounding Restormel.

The Castle lies a mile or so to the north of Lostwithiel. The site is a naturally strong one with a steep slope on three sides. Little trace now remains of the bailey on the western side of the castle, but the circular keep is in a fine state of preservation. Originally the buildings would have been of timber construction, the oldest stonework being the gate tower, dating from about 1100. Possibly a century later the curtain wall was built, eight feet thick and surmounted by a battlemented parapet; against the inner face of this wall a range of domestic buildings was later constructed. Seen from the railway in the valley below, the castle looks like a crown surmounting the hill, and has the perfect air of medieval romance, particular in the half-light of a late afternoon in winter.

The sensitive visitor standing within the walls of the now silent castle might conjure up a picture of the visits of the Black Prince in 1354 and 1365, the stonework resounding to voices raised in battle at Crecy; or again he might move forward in time and recreate the final chapter in the castle's history in August 1644, when Royalist forces captured it from Essex's Parliamentary army. From the ramparts we gain much the same splendid view that the medieval guards must have seen; true, the railway was not then part of the scene, and Lostwithiel less extensive, but the river would still thread its way through the valley south to the sea, and the wind would stir the woods and blow fresh against these same stones.

A mile up the river from Restormel is Respryn Bridge, and up the hill to the west lie the woods and park of Lanhydrock, one of the finest houses in Cornwall. Originally in the hands of the Augustinian Priory at Bodmin, the history of the manor really begins in 1620 when it was bought by Richard Robartes, a banker and merchant in Truro who had acquired his wealth in the tin and timber trades. He became Baron Robartes in 1624 (for which he paid £10,000 to the Duke of Buckingham) and began the building of the house. He continued to live in Truro until his death in 1634 and his son John completed the building work.

The Robartes family were leading Parliamentarians, and during the eclipse of their cause in Cornwall Lanhydrock passed into Royalist hands. However, this was only a temporary inconvenience and, returned to his estate, Robartes developed it by planting the fine avenue leading up the hill from the entrance near Respryn Bridge and finishing the building of the gatehouse at its head. The Restoration of the Monarchy in 1660 did not mean the end of the family fortunes: far from it, for Robartes made his peace with the restored monarchy, was made Lord Lieutenant of Ireland and became Earl of Radnor. The house remained in the Robartes family for three centuries, and in 1953 the seventh Lord Clifden gave it to the National Trust who now maintain it. In about 1780 the east wing of the former quadrangle was removed, exposing the other three wings to the sun and leaving the gatehouse isolated. This granite barbican now stands in dignified and solitary state at the end of the sycamore avenue. In 1881 fire devastated the house, much of which apart from the north wing and the porch was destroyed.

As a result of the rebuilding—to the former plan and entirely of local materials—the house we see today is partly a survival of the seventeenth century and also an evocation of the country-house life of the turn of the century. This atmosphere lingers particularly in the billiard room and smoking room with their photographs and mementoes. The seventeenth century lives in the north wing where fortunately the gallery on the first floor was saved from the fire. This splendid, many-windowed room runs the length of the wing, and its glory is the plaster barrel ceiling depicting Old Testament scenes, with a wealth of animal life in the smaller panels between the main designs. The house is set against a background of trees, and in contrast to the wooded park there are neat formal gardens beside the house and a shrub garden with exotic plants of many varieties.

The traveller from Lanhydrock to St Austell finds himself on high ground, and the road at one point offers a magnificent view over Lostwithiel, with the river winding its way south in the distance, and the wooded valley north of the town. We are now entering the parish of Lanlivery, until the fifteenth century the mother church of Lostwithiel. In the north of the parish is the great granite outcrop of Helman Tor, whose long rugged outline is a notable feature of the landscape, particularly seen from the west. The commanding view from the Tor well rewards the effort of the climb. To the north is Bodmin and its valley, on the south-western horizon the gaunt outline of the Hensbarrow massif and the china clay mountains; immediately below us to the east stretches the mysterious scrub of Red Moor, and beyond it the rolling country east of the Fowey, with the headlands above Lantic Bay bulking in the distant haze. Southwards the country drops away to the parish of Luxulyan, and over the shoulder of a hill we can just see the pinnacles of Lanlivery church tower standing up like ears.

The stately tower of Lanlivery, nearly 100 feet high and visible over a large area, consists of massive blocks of granite, and at neighbouring Luxulyan the whole church is built of this stone. This is not surprising when we travel though the parish, since granite is part of the landscape, with several quarries in the district. Indeed the parish has given its name to a particular type of porphyry, pink spotted with black, known as luxulianite; the most famous example of this is the sarcophagus of the Duke of Wellington in the crypt of St Paul's Cathedral, which was made from a block weighing about 70 tons. A church window and a memorial in the churchyard are a reminder of the work of the Cornish architect Sylvanus Trevail, who left his Victorian mark around the county in the shape of many public buildings, including the great bulk of the Headland Hotel at Newquay.

The Luxulyan river rises on Black Moor and after flowing past the village enters the spectacular gorge of the Luxulyan valley. This inland valley is narrow and strewn with enormous granite boulders. A road winds along part of the valley keeping company with the stream, a road much better suited for walking than for driving, not only for convenience but because only on foot can one properly appreciate the beauty of the scene. The vegetation is thick and luxuriant, and the stream sings its way past rocks and under the branches of trees which overhang it. At one point the valley is spanned by the spectacular granite Treffry viaduct, an exceedingly fine composition like a Cornish Pont du Gard.

Eventually the river reaches flatter ground by St Blazey, and makes its way to the sea at Par. Only two centuries ago the flatter ground inland from Par was an estuary, as far inland as St Blazey bridge, and the coastline was quite different. Indeed Tywardreath—'the house on the strand'—now lies well inland. Before the Reformation the Benedictine Priory at Tywardreath was a thriving monastic house, but by the time of the Dissolution reform was overdue, and the lax little community was dispersed; the slate tomb of Prior Colyns is now in the parish church. We are now on the west side of the peninsula where Essex's army was caught in 1644. If we were to follow the coast path from Fowey westwards, leaving the woods of Menabilly inland, we should reach the southern extremity of the peninsula at Gribbin Head. This headland, owned by the National Trust and crowned with its red and white day mark, constitutes the eastern end of St Austell Bay, and from the path above the cliffs we have a fine panorama of the bay.

Black Head, the site of an ancient promontory castle, guards the western end of the bay. From here the cliffs stretch north to the inlet of Porthpean, the hill behind crowned with the woods of Penrice. Work and leisure rub shoulders around the bay, with the holiday camp at Duporth close to the little harbour at Charlestown, and the stretch of sands at Carlyon Bay a near neighbour to the port of Par. Beyond the scene of busy activity the little fishing village of Polkerris lies tucked under the protecting arm of our headland. Inland from Carlyon Bay, beyond the golf course, the spire of Par church stands up on its hill looking down over the wooded park of the late Georgian Tregrehan house. But from our viewpoint what chiefly takes the eye is the astonishing landscape inland behind St Austell: the world of china clay.

St Austell itself is one of Cornwall's principal urban areas, but this represents a comparatively recent expansion of a small community. At the western end of the present town three valleys meet, providing a natural site for a settlement, and in the narrow valley leading north towards Bodmin is the ancient well of Menacuddle. But modern St Austell began to develop with the rise of Polgooth mine, whose old workings still dominate the horizon west of the town. This mine was at the height of its production at the end of the eighteenth century, and when it declined in the 1840's other mines were active in the eastern part of the parish, in addition to the rise of the china clay industry. This industrial activity, together with the development of the southern route through Cornwall and the arrival of the railway in 1859 established St Austell as a town of importance.

The parish was always a large one, and its importance is reflected by the church of Holy Trinity, a large building, now mainly of fifteenth-century date, with a particularly fine exterior. The glory of the church is the tower, of Somerset type, like that a few miles west at Probus, and faced with Pentewan stone. Apart from the ornate decorative carving of the tower, each face has saints in niches, and on the west side—best seen in the light of the evening sun—is a wealth of carving, pride of place being given to a representation of the Holy Trinity itself. Other notable buildings include the simple and sturdy Quaker Meeting House of 1829 and the Italianate Town Hall of 1844, while finest of all is the White Hart Hotel south of the church. Built as the town house of Charles Rashleigh of Duporth, this contains paintings and wall-paper of unusual interest, and helps to compensate for a lack of buildings of character, a natural result of the recent and rapid growth of the town.

What St Austell definitely does reflect is the prosperity of the china clay industry, which has stamped its personality on the landscape in no uncertain way. The white mountains of the granite uplands in the centre of the county are not depressing, like the spoil heaps of most industries; indeed they have their own beauty, especially after a snowfall when they really resemble a mountain range. For someone not native to the area, a journey through the heart of the clay district is quite amazing. Everything is arid, hard and—above all—white; it is a world of its own, almost an alien planet. It is hard to believe that not far distant are the woods and leafy lanes, the valleys, cliffs and beaches we associate with Cornwall: we might be a thousand miles away. But this landscape is now part of the Cornish scene, and an important part, ever since the industry first started to develop.

The production of porcelain originated in China well over a thousand years ago. When it became known in Europe, there was keen competition to discover the formula, but both the constituents and the methods of production were a jealously guarded secret. Early in the eighteenth century a French Jesuit missionary in China wrote an account of porcelain manufacture in that country, and identified the essential constituents. These were *petuntse*, or china stone, and *kaolin*, or china clay, named after the 'high ridge' (Kao-lin) in China where it was found. What was not realised at this stage was that these were granite products, kaolin being decomposed felspar, combined with mica and quartz, from which it had to be separated.

It was about the middle of the eighteenth century that the first discovery of deposits in Cornwall was made by William Cookworthy. His first experiments were not in the St Austell area but at Tregonning Hill in the parish of Germoe. However, subsequent investigations at St Stephens convinced him that the Hensbarrow Downs area contained much larger deposits, and of a better quality. Eventually Staffordshire potters, led by Wedgwood, took advantage of the newly discovered source, and cargoes of clay began to leave Cornwall for the Midlands; it was always more of an economic proposition to transport the clay rather than to try to establish potteries in Cornwall.

The process of extraction has been much improved since the days when clay was dug out and taken to a stream to be washed, days when pits were only worked to a depth of about ten feet after which drainage became too great a problem. Now the pits are enormous excavations, hundreds of feet deep, and since the valuable clay accounts for only about ten per cent of the material removed, the tips of waste material, or 'burrows', have grown increasingly larger. Efforts are now being made to landscape these mountains, and to encourage growth such as rhododendrons and lupins to cover them. Down in the pits power-hoses are directed against the side, and the material dislodged passes through a series of processes of separation and drying, until it is ready to be transported, either to other parts of the country or abroad.

The transport of china clay is a story in itself. A man of enterprise in the earlier days was Charles Rashleigh, born at the family house of Menabilly in 1774—the same Rashleigh who built the

White Hart Hotel; his name is commemorated at Mount Charles on the eastern side of St Austell, where he built miners' cottages. In 1791 he began the work of converting the beach of West Polmear into a harbour, again enshrining his name—Charlestown. Boats had formerly discharged and embarked cargoes on the beach, not always without disaster, and the construction of a harbour, even in miniature as space dictated, made a great difference to the handling of the outgoing china clay and the incoming coal. The work took several years, including a pier for loading and unloading, lock-gates, warehouses and other buildings; however, the result was a flourishing little port, which at one time handled the bulk of the china clay traffic.

Further west, beyond Black Head, a stream runs down from the west of St Austell to the coast at Pentewan, and this was the scene of another development scheme, largely the work of Sir Christopher Hawkins of Trewithen. An already existing harbour was rebuilt, and in 1829 a railway was laid down the valley, extending four miles. Clay brought to St Austell was sent down the line by gravity, the wagons returning by horse power; engines were introduced in 1874 but the last train ran in 1918. Two factors were responsible. One was the continual problem of preventing the harbour from becoming silted up, and unfortunately the works which the port served were themselves responsible for choking it with the waste material which the streams carried with them. The other factor was increasing competition from the ports at the eastern end of the clay district.

As the area of clay working spread north to St Dennis and Roche, attention turned to the north coast, particularly the newly developed harbour at Newquay. It was the remarkable character J. T. Austen, or J. T. Treffry as he was later known, who first started work on the harbour at Par, originally for the benefit of his granite and copper interests. From its beginning in 1829, it grew until it was handling more trade than Charlestown, aided by the coming of the railway.

But Treffry's plans were not limited to creating a harbour. In 1842 he built a canal up the Luxulyan river valley to Pont's Mill, then a horse-drawn tramroad to Molinnis near Bugle, to serve the granite quarries and the eastern part of the clay district. This involved an inclined plane worked by a water-wheel, and the construction of the Treffry viaduct, which carried the tramroad and a watercourse for 200 yards over the Luxulyan valley at a height of

100 feet. In 1838 he had bought the harbour at Newquay, and begun a line to the north-west of the clay district, starting with a cable-worked incline from the harbour and a viaduct over the Trenance valley. In 1850 Treffry himself died, but the network was developed, and in 1874 a single-line track from Fowey to Newquay was opened for goods traffic, with a new section through the Luxulyan valley at a lower level. This route skirts the clay district on the east and north, and is now active in the holiday season linking Newquay with Par on the main line.

The opening of the railway from Lostwithiel to Fowey in 1869 brought an increase in the cargoes handled at that port. The advantage of Fowey over Par lies in the deep water anchorage at the jetties north of the town; the harbour at Par has been developed so as to accommodate more vessels at one time but it lacks the depth to take the larger ocean-going ships. A recent development is the conversion of the railway between Par and Fowey (including a tunnel) into a road entirely for the use of vehicles engaged in the industry.

Like any industry, china clay has had its ups and downs; a boom in the 1850's was followed by the depression of the 1870's, succeeded in its turn by a recovery in the next decade. In the early days, each pit required only a small work force, often indeed being a family affair, but gradually companies became bigger and local families with initiative and enthusiasm controlled affairs. This century has seen the amalgamation of companies. Under the direction of English China Clays the industry has flourished, and is now a vital part of Cornwall's economy, 75 per cent of the output being for the export market.

Only a small proportion of china clay and china stone is now used for the production of porcelain, the largest use being the manufacture of paper; various qualities of clay are produced, and other products requiring it include paints, leather, rubber, linoleum, inks, dyes, artists' materials, textile fabrics, fertiliser, cosmetics and toothpaste. A few pits are worked in other parts of Cornwall, but the vast bulk of the clay comes from this area north of St Austell. It is now almost impossible to imagine what the district must have been like before the industry started. Several tin mines were worked in the area—indeed in many instances the clay industry took over abandoned tin mines, including tools and the labour force, though generally the tin miner considered clay working beneath his dignity. The villages in the area consist usually of rows of nineteenth-century and later houses, with one or two older settlements worth noticing.

On the main road between St Austell and Newquay lies the village of St Stephens with its large church, its exterior built of granite; this replaced the original Norman church, whose font with engaging animals and faces is worth seeing. From the old village the roads climb the downs between the clay works, through industrial villages such as Treviscoe, Nanpean and Foxhole, and, working our way round the north-west flank of the white world, we climb to the village of St Dennis. The village with its houses, institutes and chapels is dominated by a low tor, crowned with a church. The hill-top is a naturally defensive position and consequently is the site of an early camp, with two circles of ramparts, the inner of which is now represented by the churchyard wall. The very name may originate in the Cornish word for a fort—*dinas*.

To the east of St Dennis can be seen the church of the neighbouring village of Roche. Here is another fine Norman font with carved heads, snakes and lilies, and an ancient cross, one of several in the parish. The name derives from the huge outcrop of schorl known as Roche Rock, just outside the village. On its own this massive rock would surely qualify as one of the wonders of the Cornish world, but what makes it seem even more fantastic is the medieval hermitage which appears to grow out of the rock itself. The building, dating from the early fifteenth century, consisted of a room for an anchorite or chaplain, with the chapel itself on the floor above, dedicated—on its lofty perch—to St Michael. More masonry was added in a later century for temporary occupation, but the bulk of what we see is original, and the thought of its construction and the handling of the granite blocks takes the breath away.

Here at Roche we are at the northern extremity of the clay uplands, and to the north-east the country drops away towards Bodmin and the central valleys. To the east is the unmistakable outline of Helman Tor, gaunt and rugged, while to the south can be seen the Beacon, the summit of Hensbarrow Downs. Beyond this, the highest point in the whole of this area of Cornwall, only four or five miles as the crow flies, lies St Austell, the capital of the clay kingdom.

But what a world lies between: a land of bustling activity, a ceaseless process of extracting clay from the depths of the Cornish earth and starting it on journeys to all parts of the world. And amid the activity of the present stand witnesses of the past, pits no longer echoing to the sounds of men at work, but silent, filled with water of a startling green intensity, reflecting the white cones towering above them. Eventually, one assumes, the whole industry will come to an end, the extraction of china clay will be a thing of the past, and the streams will cease to run white like milk. But man has made an ineradicable mark on Hensbarrow Downs, and the white world will never be the same again.

FIVE

North Mid-Cornwall

The county town of Bodmin occupies a commanding site, looking towards the Fowey estuary to the south and the Camel estuary to the north-west, and it acquired early importance as a trading centre. This was despite the fact that it lay away from the main routes until the road across Bodmin Moor was constructed. Later the main railway also left it aside, following the River Fowey along the wooded Glynn valley, though the railway from Bodmin to Wadebridge, following the valley of the Camel, was in fact one of the earliest lines to be opened in the country.

Bodmin's chief importance in the Middle Ages was as an ecclesiastical centre. The Celtic St Guron was the first on the scene with his cell and holy well in the valley, but in the 6th century the chief of the Cornish saints, Petroc, moved here from Padstow and founded a Priory.

Religious authority reigned supreme until the Dissolution, but now hardly anything survives of the Priory which for centuries dominated the life of the town, nor of the Franciscan Friary founded in the thirteenth century. But what Bodmin still does possess is the largest parish church in the county, containing a noble monument to Prior Thomas Vivian, an extravagantly carved Norman font—the finest in the county—and the Bodmin Casket. This recalls an incident in 1177 when the bones of St Petroc, newly moved from the parish church to a shrine in the monastery, were taken to Brittany by a member of the community with reasons for resentment against the house. They were presented to a monastery in Brittany, but an expedition backed by the King himself set out to retrieve the holy relics, and they were returned in this ivory casket and replaced in the parish church.

The ecclesiastical buildings—including the now ruined chapel of St Thomas Becket close to the church—were all in the valley at the eastern end of the town. At Mount Folly, the square in the town centre, are the Assize Courts; the severity of the granite facing is appropriate. Perhaps the grim aspect of the old Bodmin gaol is also appropriate to its original function. Until 1862, after which executions were no longer public, these events always attracted large crowds, particularly after the coming of the railway, and local tradesmen took full advantage. The building was abandoned as a prison in the early years of this century. If the past seems oppressive in this ancient town, climb the windswept Beacon above the town with its obelisk set up in 1856 to commemorate Sir Walter Raleigh Gilbert, a divisional commander in the Sikh Wars. Here is a splendid view over the town and away to the woods and the Camel valley.

If we leave Bodmin and follow the road for Wadebridge, we descend a steep hill which brings us over a single-track railway line and down to the River Camel. This railway follows the course of the river upstream for several miles through picturesque wooded country as far as Wenford Bridge. Dating from 1834, it is purely a mineral line serving the china clay works and the De Lank granite quarries. Just beyond the point where the railway crosses our road, it meets the line from Bodmin to Wadebridge, which continues to follow the course of the Camel through more wooded country to Wadebridge at the head of the estuary.

The water of the Camel and its tributaries sees considerable variety on its journey from source to sea. It begins life on high moorland, sings its way through leafy valleys and loses its high spirits on reaching the estuary where it wanders in a leisurely way among the sand bars, eventually out into the Atlantic. Largest of the tributaries is the Allen—formerly the Laine, since Allen is another old name for the Camel itself. This rises near Delabole, and accompanies the main road from St Teath to St Kew Highway along a most attractive wooded valley, meeting the main stream just below Sladesbridge.

A couple of miles or so higher another tributary joins the Camel, this time from the other side; the streams from the parishes of St Wenn and Withiel join to flow under Ruthernbridge and so into the main river. These streams come from the central watershed of Cornwall's spine; within a few hundred yards, under the shadow of the great Iron Age fort of Castle-an-Dinas, rise streams which flow south to become the River Fal. The pretty De Lank River in its upper reaches flows through very lonely country in the heart of Bodmin Moor, though the numerous stone circles at Fernacre and on the shoulders of Garrow Tor show that in prehistoric times this was a populous area. The stream is spanned by several clapper bridges, constructed probably in medieval times of huge granite slabs laid on pillars in rough but very serviceable style. It later passes the De Lank granite quarries, which supplied the stone for the Eddystone lighthouse, and after flowing under the Wenford Bridge railway joins the main river.

The Camel itself rises several miles above Camelford, the main settlement on its course, a thirteenth-century market town which has not developed much beyond its one street of grey houses and shops along the main road from Launceston to Wadebridge. The parish church of Lanteglos lies outside the town, while a mile to the south-east stands the lonely little church of St Adwenna at Advent, set in isolation amid the fields, not far from the Devil's Jump, a mysterious place where two granite piles stand on either side of a ravine.

The Camel continues on its way, receiving the stream from Crowdy Reservoir and the clay works on Stannon Down, and entering a steep wooded valley between the parishes of Michaelstow and St Breward. Most of the medieval bridges spanning the Camel have been rebuilt following the dramatic day in July 1847 when after a cloudburst on Davidstow Moor a wall of water rushed down the valley carrying all before it. Only Helland Bridge proved strong enough to resist the onslaught, and remains today one of the finest medieval bridges in the county.

St Breward is a bleak settlement with its stormswept church at the northern end of the village. Norman in origin, there is little of the early work now to be seen since the ravages of J. P. St Aubyn's restoration. If we travel the four miles or so to neighbouring Blisland, the contrast is remarkable. Here—unusual for Cornwall—is a homely village green, set about with ash and elm, surrounded by manor house and granite cottages. Granite also is the church south of the green, dedicated to St Proteus and St Hyacinth.

One's first sight of the interior is breath-taking. For here in the early years of the century F. C. Eden worked a miracle of reconstruction. Granite pillars rise from the slate floor to the barrel roof

1 *Above* Lanhydrock House　2 *Below* Trerice Manor

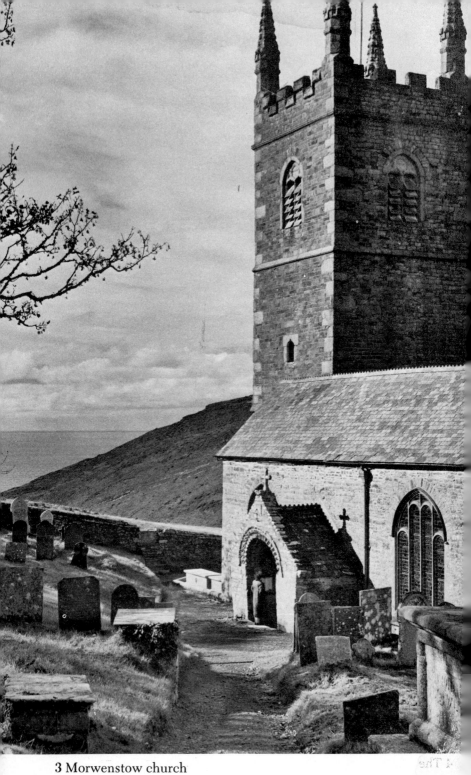

3 Morwenstow church

4 The Cheesewring

5 *Above* Polperro **6** *Below* Mending nets, Mevagissey

7 A china clay pit near St Austell

8 *Above* Restormel Castle   9 *Below* Rough Tor

10 *Above* Respryn Bridge   **11** *Below* Wadebridge

12 Truro Cathedral

13 *Above* The harbour, St. Ives   **14** *Below* The harbour, Falmouth

15 *Left* Medieval cross, Lostwithiel churchyard **16** *Above* Monument in Mevagissey church **17** *Below* Base of the rood screen, St Levan church

18 Crackington Haven

19 Abandoned engine-house, Rinsey Head

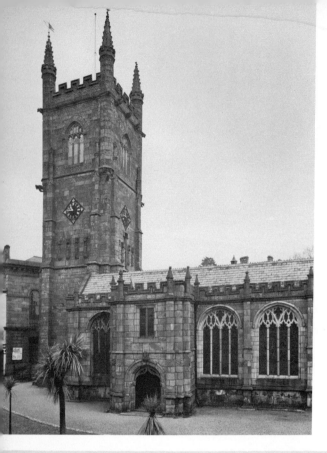

20 St Austell church

21 Gunwalloe church

22 St Michael's Mount

23 The Market House, Penzance

24 Sennen Cove

25 Land's End and the Longships Lighthouse

with its bosses, and the Georgian style pulpit looks down on old carved benches. In the sanctuary is an Italianate altar, but wonder of wonders is the screen which runs full length across the church, richly carved and ornamented and bearing the figures of the rood. Here is an insight into the atmosphere of a medieval church, where our worshipping forefathers fell to their knees before the sacred mysteries.

At the head of the Camel estuary is the market town and former port of Wadebridge. It lies between the two churches which serve it, Egloshayle on the north bank with its Georgian and Victorian houses, and St Breock, picturesquely situated in a valley beyond the river. The ancient name of Wade is a reminder that there was originally a ford at this point on the northern route into Cornwall, with a chapel at each side of the passage. In the later fifteenth century the river was bridged between these chapels, largely due to the efforts of the vicar of Egloshayle. This splendid structure, by far the longest bridge in the county with its 17 arches, has had to be widened more than once to accommodate more traffic. The chapels have now completely vanished, but then Wadebridge itself has changed considerably since medieval times.

With the silting up of the estuary the large boats which formerly came up to the wharves were denied passage. However, the railway was an early arrival here, and formerly ran along the south side of the estuary to Padstow. The town is now a market centre, the major event in the year being the annual show of the Royal Cornwall Agricultural Association on the permanent showground at the top of the hill on the main road to St Columb.

In the summer Wadebridge has to contend with a trail of traffic, most of it making for the holiday area east of the Camel estuary, but before we follow the lure of the sea it is worth exploring the parish of St Kew. The little village lies beside the stream which flows past Chapel Amble and out into the estuary. A handsome Georgian vicarage stands beside the church, which contains a fine Elizabethan pulpit, richly ornamented, and a notable array of medieval stained glass, including a window of the Passion and part of a window of the Tree of Jesse. Of much earlier date is a stone with one of the rare examples in Cornwall of Ogham writing, a script associated chiefly with south-west Ireland.

Though the main road now crosses the Camel at Wadebridge, there was in the Middle Ages a regular route to the north, keeping to the high ground from Delabole to St Endellion and down to the river at Rock. Here the ferry took passengers to Padstow immediately across the water. The character of the river has now changed, and where the trading vessels plied the estuary is now a haven for small pleasure boats.

The church of St Endellion, crouching low beside the road to ride out the gales which blow over this plateau above the north coast, is well preserved and cared for, a fine setting for the annual music festival which takes place here. Catacleuse stone from the quarries beyond the Camel was employed for the holy water stoup by the south door and for the fine altar tomb with its ogee niches. There are three small harbours in the parish, with Port Gaverne the most easterly and in the west Port Quin. Disaster struck the community here at the end of the last century when the fishermen were all lost at sea, and the village became neglected and decayed. The main harbour of Port Isaac, with its precipitous hills, took advantage of its situation in a gap in the cliffs and the fishing community here flourished.

The high cliffs continue westward to Pentire Point with its unimpeded westerly aspect. The Rumps headland has one of the best examples of a promontory cliff castle, in a position which must have been almost impregnable. Much of this magnificent cliff scenery is in the hands of the National Trust, and safe from the developer: not so around the corner on the east side of the Camel estuary where the popular holiday resorts have spread along the coast. This is the Cornwall close to the heart of Sir John Betjeman, who has captured its spirit with particular appeal, the spray glistening on the black slate and the cry of the gulls echoing over the bladder-wrack, the sea-pink and mesembryanthemum.

We are now in the parish of St Minver which—remarkably for Cornwall—possesses two churches with spires. The churchtown on St Minver Highlands contains the parish church, whose spire was reconstructed in the nineteenth century; St Enodoc church needed greater restorative work, after being dug out of the sands, so that the Victorian hand lies rather hard on its interior. It would be difficult, however, to deny the attraction of its setting, on a golf course in the shadow of Bray Hill, a holy island set about with tamarisks within sound of the sea rolling in on Daymer Bay.

From Rock we may cross to Padstow by the passenger ferry or take the road around the head of the estuary and approach from the south. From Wadebridge the road keeps to the high ground and from St Issey descends to the village of Little Petherick at the head of its creek. The medieval church has gone, and what we see now is essentially a mid-Victorian building, but this contains more of interest than its exterior suggests. In 1898 the patronage came into the hands of Athelstan Riley, and he brought here Sir Ninian Comper who continued the work of decoration so that the church became a place of Anglo-Catholic pilgrimage. The screen and loft are Comper's work, as are the high altar and a reredos. Athelstan Riley collected and gave to the church several vestments and items of plate, and his heart now lies within the Chantry Chapel built to commemorate his wife, with a fine bronze monument in her memory. Here beside the busy road is an atmosphere of mystery, of quiet care and devotion.

The dedication of Little Petherick is to St Petroc, and Padstow—or Petroc Stow—was the site of the first monastery of this chief of our Cornish saints. He is said to have landed after his journey from Ireland on the opposite shore of the estuary at Trebetherick; there he wrought a miracle by striking water from the rock. Afterwards he crossed the water and settled to a life of austerity at Padstow before setting off on further missionary travels, returning eventually to die in this territory on which his memory is so impressed.

Medieval Padstow came under the protection and control of the Church, in the persons of the Priors of Bodmin, and developed as the principal port on this coast. Ecclesiastical influence, however, did not prevent the annual observance of the May Day celebrations. The houses decked with greenery, the Hobby Horse reigned supreme from early morning, and people treasured in their memory for another year the song of rejoicing for the annual miracle of fertility and rebirth. In former centuries the festival was the property of the local people; now, of course, in an age of instant communication and ease of travel, its fame is world-wide.

The age of Church domination came to a rude end in the sixteenth century when, as in so many other instances at the time of the Dissolution of the Monasteries, secular hands took over. In the case of Padstow, the Prideaux family became the chief figures, largely thanks to the forethought of the last Prior of Bodmin and his steward Nicholas Prideaux, who acquired lands and tithes and established the family at Prideaux Place. The descendants of the family have lived ever since in this house dominating the town and looking across the estuary; it remains a very fine Elizabethan

house, with a deer park, and possesses a rarity in its hall, in
Strawberry Hill Gothic.

The town occupies a cramped position, and therefore has not
suffered from over-development, as a result retaining its attraction. A variety of styles is evident in the buildings surrounding the
harbour: red brick, stone and slate-hung houses. The large and
well-restored church lies up the hill on the road out of the town,
with its fine catacleuse font and its array of Prideaux monuments.

The home of the catacleuse stone is only a few miles away, at
Cataclews Point in the adjoining parish of St Merryn; the church
here naturally has a good deal of this dark grey stone, notably a
fifteenth-century arcade of seven bays. From Stepper Point with
its day mark at the entrance to the Camel estuary the coast contains some grand cliff scenery and magnificent stretches of golden
sand such as Harlyn Bay looking north, and Constantine Bay and
Treyarnon Bay beyond the headland facing west. Here amid the
holiday scene are evidences of earlier centuries, for at Constantine
Bay are the remains of a medieval chapel and at Harlyn Bay an
Iron Age burial site. A museum now houses the findings from this
site, where over a hundred burials took place, more than 2,000
years ago; the stern little cemetery by the sea makes modern
tourism seem very much a parvenu.

The central point on this stretch of coast is Trevose Head,
stretching out its lighthouse north and west, full in the face of all
weathers and commanding magnificent views of the headlands in
each direction. One of the characteristic features of the coastal
scenery of Cornwall is the succession of bays and headlands. This
is the result of the unceasing action of the sea on different types of
stone; the harder rocks now stand out as headlands, while the sea
has worn away the less resistant stone to form the inlets, the bays
and coves so typical of both coasts. It is noticeable too how much
the sea has worked on the coastline from a westerly direction, all
this happening of course over countless centuries before historical
times.

The National Trust owns a stretch of this westward-facing coast
at Park Head, and also at Bedruthan Steps with its procession of
great rocks rising in giant strides from the sea. Beyond Mawgan
Porth the coast sweeps away along the sands of Watergate Bay to
the holiday playground of Newquay. Inland on the plateau
behind the cliffs are the runways of St Eval and St Mawgan, the
airfields which are man's latest contribution to the landscape. St

Eval church stands marooned in lonely isolation, a landmark to airmen as well as to generations of seamen passing on their way up and down the Bristol Channel.

Between the two airfields lies the wooded Vale of Lanherne or Mawgan, with its little river running down to the sea at Mawgan Porth, where 1,000 years ago existed a Dark Age village, before the advancing sand drove the inhabitants inland. A couple of miles up the stream is the village of Mawgan-in-Pydar. In contrast to St Eval, the church here is in a beautiful wooded coombe, set amongst cottages and the manor house. Much of the church dates from the thirteenth century, with an aisle added and the tower enlarged in the fifteenth century, and a notable feature of the dark interior is the tall screen. Close by the church is the manor house of Lanherne, in the sixteenth century the home of the Arundell family. Queen Anne extensions were added to the Elizabethan building, and since 1794 it has been a convent, originally accommodating Carmelite nuns who had fled from France and found sanctuary here.

In the late sixteenth century Lanherne had greater significance than merely being the seat of the Arundells: it was the centre of Catholicism in the county. After the Papal Bull of 1570 excommunicating Elizabeth, adherence to the old faith became dangerous. The Arundell family became closely involved by marriage with the Tregians of Golden; at his manor house beside the Fal just above Tregony Francis Tregian took into his household the young and zealous Cuthbert Mayne, trained as a seminary priest at Douai. In the guise of a steward Mayne ministered to both families at Golden and Lanherne until the summer day in 1577 when the Sheriff of Cornwall descended on Golden, searched the house and found Mayne with incriminating evidence. Neither family was prepared to conform, and under the severe recusancy laws suffered the heavy financial penalties which impoverished them. As for Mayne, his execution at Launceston set the pattern for many further such martyrdoms for the old faith. After adorning the gate of Launceston Castle, his head was preserved as a sacred relic at Lanherne, the house which he had known and served in the peaceful wooded valley beside the stream.

We can see the Arundell monuments if we follow the Vale of Lanherne upstream to St Columb Major; the south chancel aisle contains brasses in their memory. This small hill-top town grew up on the northern route through Cornwall, and the size of its church is witness to its importance in medieval times. The church was indeed considered as a candidate for cathedral status when the Cornish diocese was being formed in the nineteenth century, and is another fine setting for an annual music festival; it stands up particularly well when seen across the valley on the approach from the north. In the town itself, William White's Venetian Gothic Bank House is worth seeing, in addition to all the attractive slate-hung houses and the chapels in the main street.

As May Day is Padstow's great occasion, so in St Columb Shrove Tuesday is of special significance. For then town and country are the rival factions in the ancient sport of Hurling. Windows are boarded up, old clothes are worn, the wooden ball in its silver casing is thrown high in the air, and battle begins. Other places in the county, such as St Just, are associated with hurling, which somewhat resembles a large-scale and indisciplined game of Rugby football—itself a sport taken very seriously in Cornwall. But St Columb holds pride of place as the home of hurling, and also has associations with another honourable Cornish sport, wrestling, one of our links with Brittany. A former landlord of the Red Lion Inn was the St Keverne man James Polkinghorne, heavyweight champion of Cornwall, whose great rival was the Devon champion Abraham Cann. This was in the early nineteenth century, but the origin of 'wrastling' can be traced back to ancient times.

Pre-eminent among modern wrestlers were the Chapman family, who came from the neighbouring parish of St Wenn, where the punning inscription of the church sundial sardonically reads, 'Ye know not when'. Certainly we know not when the first fortifications were set up on the hill-top two miles away at Castle-an-Dinas, but here is the finest of all the Cornish Iron Age forts. Its position high above the Goss Moor commands the central routes across the county, and with its triple ramparts it must have dominated the whole area. From this central boss, the streams run in all directions—south to the Fal, north-east to the Camel, west to the Vale of Lanherne and to Porth near Newquay.

The roads from Bodmin and Wadebridge join at Fraddon. Skirting the western fringe of the china clay district the road to Truro turns away to the south, while the western route enters the parish of St Enoder, through Summercourt, the site of an ancient annual fair, to Mitchell. In the thirteenth century this village became the site of a weekly market as well as an annual fair. But it lacked the natural assets to permit growth and development, and became one of the many rotten boroughs so notorious in Cornwall before the Great Reform Bill.

From the main roads running west through the county several routes take the traveller to the coast and the principal centre of the holiday industry, Newquay. Evidence of very early occupation can be seen at the sites of promontory cliff castles, but now interest is mainly centred on the splendid series of beaches which lie between the headlands. Golden sands and surfing in the Atlantic rollers are the natural advantages now supported by all kinds of glittering attractions to entice and delight the holiday-maker.

Of course it was not always so. In medieval times a harbour grew up at the sheltered western end of the bay, where it still is, though few old buildings now survive. The 'new quay' was built in the sixteenth century, and Newquay it has remained, 400 years later. In the early nineteenth century the picturesque port began to attract tourists, particularly as the Napoleonic Wars put a temporary stop to Continental holidaying. The arrival of the railway (originally for industrial purposes) gave further impetus to the growth of tourism. The big hotels arose on the cliff tops, followed by innumerable smaller hotels and boarding houses, and now with the motor car and improved access from the national centres of population the town is bursting at the seams throughout the summer months.

The mother church of Newquay is St Columb Minor, on the eastern outskirts. In Newquay itself, however, is a modern church, designed in the early years of this century by Sir Ninian Comper and completed with the building of the tower in 1968. The great Scots architect has produced a fine Cornish-style building, its interior spacious and satisfying, the stained glass and rood screen impressive without being overpowering. The church also has a wide reputation for its organ, one of the finest in the county and frequently used for recitals.

To the south of Newquay is the inland parish of Newlyn East, with old mine shafts on Newlyn Downs. For 40 or so years in the mid-nineteenth century this area was Cornwall's principal lead-mining district, with the Chiverton mines working near Zelah and others on Newlyn Downs, notably East Wheal Rose. This mine was the scene of the greatest disaster in Cornish mining history in 1846 when a cloudburst resulted in the flooding of the mine with the loss of 40 lives; but it is also to be remembered for its great output of lead ore during a comparatively short period of working.

From the village of Newlyn East a spider's web of roads radiates, and the well-restored church sits on an island in the centre of the village, with the road running round the churchyard like a moat. Inside are monuments to the Arundells of Trerice, whose most famous representative was the stubborn defender of Pendennis Castle in the Civil War.

The manor house of Trerice in its secluded setting in a valley among Cornish elms is among the prettiest of country houses. We are fortunate to possess it; many houses of this type were either totally or partially demolished in the eighteenth and nineteenth centuries, to be replaced by grander buildings reflecting the prosperity of the owners riding on the industrial high tide. Not so at Trerice, largely due to the fact that in 1768 the house passed from the Arundell family into the ownership of families resident outside Cornwall, and as a result was not developed. It became a National Trust property in 1953, and the visitor can now see an elegant and well balanced Elizabethan house, carefully maintained and in good order.

From the south-east we can see the two main fronts of the house. It commands an easterly aspect, with the porch in the centre of an E-shaped façade, the courtyard now laid out with elegant lawns. To the left of the porch is the great window of the Hall, its 24 lights comprising 576 panes of glass, much of it original. The gables present a remarkable symmetrical pattern of scrolls and curves, unusual for Cornwall yet a very satisfying composition. On the south wall the sash windows would probably have been inserted in the nineteenth century, but the principal feature is original, the semi-circular bay lighting the Solar on the first floor.

From the porch we enter the Hall in the usual way by means of a screens passage. The Hall is a magnificent room, lit by its fine window, rising through two floors to a remarkable plaster ceiling. Steps lead down from the Hall to the lower room of the south wing on the level of the medieval building; this room, the Library, was at one period converted into two smaller rooms, but has now been restored to the original plan.

A staircase leads to the upper floor of the south wing, the former Solar of the Tudor house, now the Drawing Room. This is another splendid room, with a barrel ceiling even grander than the ceiling of the Hall. With its southerly aspect and large bay window the room is wonderfully bright, and we can imagine the family sitting by the fire or in the window bay with its view over the garden and the wooded valley beyond. On the west side a gallery runs the length of the house, leading to the musicians' gallery over the screens passage, with its row of small arches giving a view down into the Hall. The furnishing of the house is mainly of a later date than the building itself, the bulk of it eighteenth-century, but the house itself has hardly changed since its construction four centuries ago. Here, tucked away from the main arteries of twentieth-century life, we can recapture the spirit of the Elizabethan Cornish gentry.

Between Trerice and the village of Newlyn East run streams which flow into the Gannel, just to the west of Newquay. In medieval times there was a thriving port here, the only sizeable inlet between Hayle and the Camel, but it suffered the usual north coast fate and became choked with sand. Crantock, which occupies the west side of the estuary, has consequently long ceased to be the port it was in the Middle Ages. The church was ruinous in the nineteenth century but was sensitively restored by Edmund Sedding. Beyond the modern screen, with its figures carved by peasants of Oberammergau, the chancel is unusually large, because before the religious upheaval of the sixteenth century this was a collegiate church, established as such in the early thirteenth century.

Following the coastal footpath brings us to the headland of Pentire Point West, at the entrance to the Gannel, and round by the sheltered sandy beach of Porth Joke to Kelsey Head where the remains of another cliff castle may be seen. The path leads on to the next beach at Holywell Bay, another former little port, in the parish of Cubert, whose church tower with its little broach spire is a landmark over a wide area. Before bringing us to Perranporth the coast path here unfortunately has to turn inland for a detour owing to the army's occupation of Penhale Sands.

The parish church of Perranzabuloe was rebuilt at the beginning of the nineteenth century, a mile or more from the centre of population. The road winds down a hill, along one of several coombes which lead to Perranporth. Here the little streams meet and flow out to the sea, losing themselves in the Atlantic surf which rolls in along a two-mile front of sand. Perranporth a century ago was a small village. With the coming of the railway it became popular as a holiday resort and grew a crop of boarding-houses. Now, its mines derelict, and despite the closure of the railway, it plays host to an invasion of thousands, who throng its beach, holiday camps and car parks throughout the summer months.

From the little town with its shops, hotels and boating lake the beach extends northwards, and behind it the dunes spread in a motionless sea of troughs and crests crowned with marram grass. North of the golf links sprawl the holiday camps, but here the present rubs shoulders with the past in a remarkable way. In a dip beyond the caravans stands what appears to be an ugly concrete structure like a miniature aircraft hangar; yet this building houses remains of great antiquity—St Piran's Oratory. From early medieval times, if not from the lifetime of St Piran himself, these walls with their altar and doorway have survived, largely buried by the shifting sands. Lost for centuries, the oratory came to light in 1835, and the protective cover was built early in this century. In former times this was good agricultural land until the advance of the sand. The dunes claimed this church and its successor, built not far away beside a plain round-headed cross. This accounts for the rebuilding well inland, St Piran in Sabulo, St Piran in the Sands.

Not that St Piran would have approved: proximity to the water's edge seems to have been characteristic of the churches founded by the Celtic missionaries. It was natural for them to start their preaching where they landed, to set up a cross and establish a site which would eventually be venerated and where a church would be built. So we find the beautiful settings of St Just in Roseland and St Winnow lapped by the waters of the Fal and the Fowey, or Gunwalloe within sound of the sea on Mount's Bay. This also helps to explain why many of the churches in Cornwall are located away from the centre of population, which may have grown up at a meeting of ancient routes or at a fishing haven. Later perhaps these would be equipped with a chapel-of-ease, with the parish church and its little 'churchtown' away over the fields.

St Piran also gives his name to the 'plan-an-gwary' known as St Piran's Round, on the road from Perranporth to Goonhavern. At first sight like a fortified castle, this is in fact a circular open-air theatre, surrounded by turf banks rising to about nine feet. It is the best known of these rounds, which occur in many places in west Cornwall: St Just has a fine example, and they are enshrined in the very names of Plain-an-Gwary near Redruth and Playing Place near Truro.

The history of St Piran's, or Perran, Round may go back to very early medieval times, but it certainly flourished in the later Middle Ages with the presentation of the Cornish Miracle Plays. The Cornish language has not left a large legacy of literature, but the miracle plays are an outstanding exception: their appeal was direct, and provided a powerful form of instruction for an illiterate people. Several lives of saints were compiled and presented, often locally, but the major work is the Ordinalia, a cycle of mystery plays comprising The Origin of the World, The Passion of Our Lord, and The Resurrection. The emphasis on the Holy Rood is the most remarkable feature of the Cornish plays, distinguishing them from all the other English cycles. The medieval audience, unaccustomed to the perpetual round of entertainment available in our time, must have gazed in wonder at the spectacle, God in his glory and demons dancing in the jaws of Hell.

If we follow the stream away from Perranporth to the south through Perrancoombe, we come close to the birthplace of one of Cornwall's most remarkable artistic figures, the painter John Opie. He was born in May 1761 at Harmony Cot, in the valley below the hamlet of Trevellas. His father wanted him to follow the family trade as a carpenter, but the boy had other ideas. At the village school he had shown an unusual aptitude for mathematics, but it was art which really fired the boy's ambition, and he began work as a travelling portrait painter. On a visit to Padstow he painted the entire Prideaux family, including the dogs and cats, and earned himself 20 guineas. Opie soon attracted the attention of John Wolcot, who took him into his house at Truro, supplied him with materials, gave him instruction and lent him pictures to copy: a succession of landscapes as well as portraits showed his developing talent.

Wolcot, 23 years his senior, had come to Cornwall as a boy on the death of his father. He lived with his uncle at Fowey and studied medicine. In 1767 he went to the West Indies, but found little chance to practise as a doctor, so returned to England to take holy orders; this soon accomplished, back to the West Indies, only to find the prospects of a living there had vanished. So he reverted to his medical career, returned to Cornwall in 1773 and settled in Truro. As Opie's reputation increased, Wolcot prompted him to raise his price. They moved to Helston, and Wolcot practised there for the next two years, and also for a time at Exeter. Then in 1780 came the decisive step: a move to London. Since Wolcot was giving up his income as a doctor, he arranged to share with Opie the profits of his painting, while for his part he introduced Opie to patrons and artists, showed his pictures and generally made him known.

Opie was now well launched in London society, and commissions rolled in. Fashionable people crowded his lodgings at Leicester Fields, eager to see 'the Cornish wonder'; his ability impressed Reynolds, who gave him encouragement and advice. His first marriage was unsuccessful; his second, to Amelia Anderson, was a much better match, but deepened the rift which had been growing between Opie and Wolcot, since Amelia actively disliked him. Perhaps Opie's criticism of Wolcot's painting was one cause of the breach, but probably financial disagreements were at the root of the trouble. At all events, by this time Wolcot had firmly laid the foundation of his own career as a satirist under the name of Peter Pindar, working on into old age, even though almost blind. He appears in his portraits as a heavy, dark man: Opie painted him at least eight times.

In 1787 Opie became an A.R.A., and a full Academician the following year: he was still only 27. In 1802 he saw in Paris the collection of paintings made by Napoleon, the pick of the art galleries of the Europe he was rapidly conquering. Three years later he became Professor of Painting at the Royal Academy, and his lectures were among the finest delivered there. Working tirelessly, he died in April 1807 and was buried in St Paul's Cathedral. Over 500 portraits and half as many other paintings witness to his genius. Dr Johnson he painted three times; among his other sitters were Burke, Fox and the poet Southey. He was renowned for an extraordinary memory and a talent for repartee; as a painter he was sincere and without artificiality. This was characteristic of Opie as a man, and perhaps his boyhood in north Cornwall had much to do with it. To the village craftsman life was simple, with little artificiality. The successful London painter cannot have forgotten Harmony Cot, the rugged cliffs and the leafy warmth of Perrancoombe in June.

SIX

Around the Fal

The broad sweep of St Austell Bay lies between the Gribbin Head and Black Head. Beyond Black Head the coast continues south to Chapel Point, enclosing Mevagissey Bay, sheltered from the prevailing westerly winds. The cliffs along this shore stretch out hostile fangs of rock into the sea, but in the one sizeable inlet has grown up the thriving port of Mevagissey. The main interest in the village is naturally centred on the harbour with its melancholy chorus of gulls and the boats moored on the placid waters. The inner harbour is protected from the swell of the English Channel by an outer pier, a lighthouse crowning the end of its southern arm.

The annual ancient service of blessing the waters is a reminder of Mevagissey's dependence on the sea. The image of St Peter, patron saint of the church and of fishermen, was once taken in solemn procession to the water's edge for the ceremony. Shipbuilding was important here, and it was around the fishing industry that the life of the community centred. As the boats brought their catch into port, the curing and packing took place in the cellars along the quay. The smell was inescapable, but it was the smell of prosperity and a flourishing trade. The nineteenth century saw the height of Mevagissey's prosperity in both fishing and boat-building, until the general decline at the end of the century. The village has retained its charm, with its rows of houses climbing the steep hills away from the harbour; there is plenty to interest the visitor—walking around the narrow streets, going out on fishing expeditions, studying the aquarium by the quay, or merely sitting on the pier in the sun watching the activity of the harbour.

The energetic walker may prefer to take the coast road south from Mevagissey through Portmellon to the neighbouring parish of Gorran. This is another example of a coastal settlement with its churchtown inland, away from the main centre of population. Gorran church itself is a large fifteenth-century building with numerous old bench-ends; around the church on its windy hill cluster the houses of the little village. The road winds down the valley to Gorran Haven, a small fishing settlement protected by a pier, with a medieval chapel—dedictated to St Just—close above the beach and the houses rising up from the haven.

Immediately to the south of Gorran is one of the finest of the south-coast headlands, the towering bulk of the Dodman, which, like many of the headlands on this stretch of coast, is fortunately protected by the National Trust. In addition to the promontory fortification there is a long defensive earthwork across the neck of the headland. The summit is crowned with a granite cross, and from here the views are tremendous: westward past the Nare Head and Gull Rock, beyond the Fal and Helford Rivers to Black Head, south of St Keverne, eastward to the Devon coastline and out to the Eddystone light, and inland to Hensbarrow Downs and the heights of Bodmin Moor. Perhaps even more awe-inspiring is the view downwards; from our vantage-point on the cliff's edge we look down a breath-catching 400 feet to the Atlantic swell ceaselessly breaking on the rocks below us. On a placid warm summer's day the scene is idyllic, with the sea a deep blue, the gulls wheeling idly below us, and the coastline stretching away into the haze in either direction. But on a day of storms the picture is utterly different: the tireless lament of the gulls sounds harsh in our ears, the salt wind assaults and buffets us, and the grey ocean is menacing and angry, attacking the rocks with relentless ferocity.

Between the Dodman and its western neighbour Pennare, or the Nare Head, lies the curve of Veryan Bay, broken by the beach at Porthluney Cove. Here the little River Luney meets the sea, having followed a southerly course from Hewas Water through Polmassick near St Ewe and finally through wooded country to the coast. Here we are in the parish of St Michael Caerhays, its church set on a hill, after the normal fashion of dedication to the archangel. Some Norman work survives here, but the usual rebuilding took place and the principal addition is the south aisle, the Lady Chapel, containing the Trevanion monuments.

Mention of the Trevanions, the family from which Byron was descended, brings us to the chief interest at Caerhays, the castle set just inland from the beach and commanding a view out to sea. The Trevanion family set their roots here in the early Middle Ages and built a charming house, which in the eighteenth century consisted of a gatehouse arch leading into a courtyard around which the low buildings were grouped, looking probably rather like Cotehele. However, this has gone, superseded by the building one sees today, dating from 1808 and designed by John Nash, whose work is typified by the conjunction of square and round towers, as at Windsor. Caerhays is a Gothic tour-de-force, with its fairytale turrets and varied levels of battlements, the grey stonework standing out against a green background of trees.

Unfortunately the great pile sat too heavily on the Trevanion family, who were ruined financially. The house was bought by the Williams family of Scorrier and rescued from decay, so that we can seen it now, almost like a theatrical set with its lake in the gardens. And wonderful gardens they are too, with rhododendrons, azaleas, camellias, all manner of shrubs and exotic tree ferns. J. C. Williams was the greatest rhododendron grower of his time, and rich enough to bring specimens from the Himalayas to his garden, set here in the steep wooded valley by the little beach.

Turning inland here we find good agricultural country, with many small streams and old farmhouses. St Ewe is an attractive little village, presided over by its church spire; the church itself is old though extensively restored, but the screen should not be missed, for its carving is among the best in Cornwall. Also among the best of its kind in the county is the Georgian rectory near the church, as in the neighbouring parish of Creed. The centre of population here lies just up the river on the main road. Indeed this is the reason for its existence, for the name Grampound developed from the 'grand pont' which here took the main road over the River Fal. The settlement by the bridge became a borough in the early fourteenth century, and was one of the most notorious rotten boroughs before parliamentary reform swept away such anachronisms. A reminder of its former importance is the delightful cupola on the little guildhall beside the main road as it climbs eastward from the river.

A few miles to the west is Probus, a village with an attractive centre where roads meet by the church. And a notable church this is, its principal exterior feature being the magnificent tower, 123 feet high, the tallest church tower in Cornwall and reminiscent of Magdalen College, Oxford. It was built in the sixteenth century, probably under the direction of Somerset masons who were creating similar splendid towers in their county at this time. The decoration is elaborate, and the whole composition very stately as it stands up proudly over the surrounding countryside, its gathered pinnacles at the top, pointing heavenward. The finest monument in the church is the eighteenth-century commemoration of Thomas Hawkins, a member of the family whose residence was just outside Probus at Trewithen. This is a delightful early Georgian house, set in a picturesquely landscaped park with woods and a lake. Great care has been taken of the gardens, splendid in spring or early summer.

The Fal flows south from Grampound, past Creed church and Golden Mill to the medieval port of Tregony. It takes a fair amount of imagination now to envisage a port here, since the river is so silted up, and many centuries have passed since boats loaded and unloaded cargoes as far up the river as this. The debris washed down by the river even destroyed the church which stood here, and which could be reached by boat. A modern bridge now carries the main road from the Roseland peninsula, while the modern village climbs the hill away from the river to the church of Cuby. The village has charm and character; it consists mainly of the one street, with a clock tower, almshouses and pleasant colour-washed houses.

South of Tregony the parish of Veryan has a variety of interest, including a tumulus at Carne which is one of the largest round barrows in Britain, probably of Bronze Age origin. The coastline includes the sands of Pendower beach, the imposing headland of the Nare Head, and the comparatively unspoilt old fishing village of Portloe. The village of Veryan itself is charming, with the church of St Symphorian in its leafy churchyard. The most noticeable features of the village are the Regency Gothic Round Houses which guard its approaches. Popular tradition declares that by their circular nature they keep out the devil; with their thatched roofs and whitewashed walls these follies certainly make an attractive and unusual welcome to the village.

We are now entering the Roseland peninsula, one of the most beautiful areas in the whole of Cornwall, far removed from the bleak moors and the towering cliffs facing the Atlantic rollers. Four parishes—Gerrans, Philleigh, St Just and St Anthony

—make up this district lying to the east of the Fal estuary and intersected by several streams and inlets. It is an area as beautiful as its name suggests, though in fact 'Roseland' means heath or promontory land. Summer seems to linger here, the air gentle and the climate as mild as anywhere in the whole country.

If we first keep to the eastern side of the peninsula, the ridgeway route brings us to Gerrans. The church with its steep octagonal spire is a landmark, especially from the sea as it stands above the harbour of Portscatho which sits snugly sheltered from the west. Formerly a mere fishing village it has developed over the years and become a favourite holiday resort, though retaining its attraction with a superb situation.

Beyond Gerrans the road makes for St Anthony, keeping to the ridgeway on the top of a narrow peninsula; for part of the way the road threads an avenue of trees which in summer create the effect of a cool green tunnel, with occasional glimpses of the sea quite close at hand. The lane winds downhill through luxuriant woods and suddenly we are at St Anthony, which lies on a little creek of the Percuil River. In early medieval times this was a monastic site, a cell of Plympton Priory. The principal building here now is Place Manor, built in the 1840's for the naval Spry family, and now a hotel. At the Dissolution of the Monasteries the church lost its chancel which was pulled down—the nave was the people's part of the church, and remained intact.

The church of St Anthony lies sheltered in its quiet valley, while just above it to the south is the magnificent headland with the lighthouse at St Anthony Head guarding the eastern entrance to the estuary of the Fal. The National Trust owns much of the coast here and the views are spectacular. At Zone Point, the southern tip of the peninsula, the open sea stretches away to the south and west, while the westward aspect commands a panorama of Falmouth Bay and the coastline of the Lizard peninsula. Immediately across the mouth of the estuary lies Falmouth, with beaches to one side and harbour to the other, separated by Pendennis Castle on its headland. Northward stretches the finest, and deepest, natural harbour in the country, Carrick Roads, with all the creeks and inlets which open from it. Innumerable rivers and streams flow into this estuary, once used by the great clippers and merchant ships from all the world's ports, now the haunt of hundreds of small boats in addition to the great vessels using the docks at Falmouth.

The town of Falmouth is a comparative newcomer, but now one of the most important in Cornwall. We shall return to it in due course, but by the landsman's route, exploring the hinterland of the great estuary with its rivers and the towns and villages which have grown up on them.

Where the Percuil River broadens out to join Carrick Roads is St Mawes, in a superbly sheltered situation facing south. With the building of the castle in the early 1540's the settlement grew and a fishing industry developed; the town became the dwelling for many connected with the sea, such as fishermen, river pilots, coopers and net-makers. St Mawes still deals very much with the sea and boats, but now largely of a different character, the harbour being a yachtsman's paradise. Sub-tropical plants flourish here, for the climate is claimed to be the mildest in the country.

It was the threat of invasion by France which resulted in the building of the castle, one of a number constructed on the orders of Henry VIII along the south coast. St Mawes and its partner on the opposite shore, Pendennis, controlled the entrance to the harbour, and by their presence enabled settlements to develop much nearer the sea than had hitherto been possible. Comparison between St Mawes and, for example, Restormel brings out all the difference between Renaissance and medieval concepts of defence. St Mawes is constructed on a clover-leaf pattern with a drawbridge approach from landward, and was not only functional but aesthetically satisfying.

St Mawes is in the parish of St Just in Roseland, occupying the western side of the peninsula, where the vegetation is as lush and exotic as at St Mawes. The church at St Just is chiefly remarkable for its setting. It stands beside its creek, tucked away out of sight of the main channel, in a jewelled setting at the foot of its churchyard, which rises precipitously in a riot of fuchsias, hydrangeas, palms and shrubs among the headstones. In the eighteenth century the site was proposed by Admiral Boscawen for the Royal Dockyard, because of the deep waters of St Just Pool; it was rejected in favour of Devonport, but was later considered for various other schemes, all of which it has so far survived. So it remains, as perfect a picture as one could hope to find, yet not so many miles from churches in bleak and harshly exposed situations, or others confronting scarred and torn industrial landscapes.

Slightly north of St Just is the head of Carrick Roads, at Turnaware Point where the River Fal emerges from its wooded slopes into the broad waters of the estuary. The traveller to the west can take advantage of the King Harry Ferry here which avoids a long and devious route by the heads of the various creeks which run inland from the main river. If one has to wait a while for the next ferry, there could scarcely be more beautiful scenery to contemplate while doing so. Thick woods run to the water's edge along most of the shore, as they must have done in even greater profusion in the days of 'King Harry'—not Henry VIII but the saintly Henry VI in whose name a chapel stood in the woods on the eastern bank.

Although the Fal gives its name to the whole river system, several rivers in fact contribute to it. The longest tidal arm is the Tresillian River, which flows into the Truro River, and this combined stream joins the Fal just above the King Harry reach. The Fal itself begins its life amid the desolation of the Goss Moor and then threads its way through the western districts of the china clay area. This has a marked influence on it, for the river which passes through Grampound and Tregony is discoloured, not a fresh clear stream but thick and cloudy. This has naturally accelerated the process of silting up which has increasingly restricted navigation of the river over the years. From Tregony the river flows through wooded country until it emerges into its own estuary where it joins the Ruan River; this is quiet and remote country, the loneliness accentuated by the mournful cry of the curlew.

Navigation by small boats was possible to Ruan Lanihorne for a while after Tregony was no longer accessible, and loading took place at a small quay. Beyond the old bridge which crosses the Fal are the exquisite Lamorran Woods, with the tiny hamlet of Lamorran beside a tidal lake set deep within the trees. This peninsula between the Fal and Truro rivers retains its unspoilt character on account of its being part of the Tregothnan estate; Lord Falmouth's woods and deer park make an unforgettable impression when seen from the river, and this part of the journey by water between Truro and Falmouth is through scenery of incomparable beauty.

Tregothnan itself with its battlements and turrets is a mansion in the grand style, commanding a magnificent view down the river. William Wilkins was the architect chiefly responsible for creating this Tudor-style house, incorporating what survived of the seventeenth-century house. The work began in 1816, and additions were made by Lewis Vulliamy in 1845. The church of St Michael Penkevil, once a collegiate church, stands by the Victorian estate houses, and contains the Boscawen family monuments, including some by Nollekens. The drive runs through woods alongside the river to the imposing entrance gates at Tresillian.

Of the streams which feed the Tresillian River the main one comes along the Ladock valley, accompanying the road and, for a short distance, the railway as well. Ladock church was restored by Street, with good Victorian work, notably Morris and Burne-Jones windows. The other streams take a more lonely course from the parish of St Erme, each following a wooded valley. St Erme church, apart from its tower, was rebuilt in 1820 by John Foulston. That this fine Plymouth architect was employed at remote St Erme in the rebuilding of church and rectory was due to the taste of the remarkable Cornelius Cardew, rector here at the beginning of the nineteenth century and Master of Truro Grammar School during the most flourishing period of its history.

The Tresillian River follows its tranquil course to the Truro River through country of exquisite beauty. The unspoilt village of St Clement clusters at the end of the road down to the river, with its church and cottages, a slate-hung schoolroom incorporating a lych-gate, and in the churchyard another example of a stone with Ogham writing. When the tide is in, the scene across the river to the woods of Tregothnan is idyllic, particularly in the light of a summer evening. The ebbing tide uncovers mudflats where innumerable wading birds fly in small flocks and call excitedly as they feed, where the brilliant blue of a kingfisher can be seen by the shaded pool and a solitary heron flaps his stately and unhurried way upstream or stands sentinel by the water's edge.

A mile or so downstream from St Clement the Tresillian River joins forces with the Truro River by the ancient ferry crossing at Malpas. The broad river curves away around the corner between its wooded banks to join the Fal, and numerous small boats ride at their moorings. Most of the houses are set on the steep hill behind us, so that our view of the river is not spoilt. In the summer months the pleasure boats from Falmouth land their passengers here when the tide is low, but on the high tides they round the bend of the Truro River and sail up to the cathedral city itself.

Arriving at Truro by the river is one of the best approaches. Another fine prospect, from a different angle, is to be seen from

the railway approach from the east; the line crosses two long viaducts and from this vantage point the traveller looks down on the
roofs and streets, with the river winding away in the distance. The
centre of the stage is occupied by the Cathedral, towering above
the buildings in its shadow; it is difficult now to envisage Truro
without it, yet it is a comparative newcomer in a town whose
history takes us back to early medieval times.

The viaducts cross the valleys of the two rivers which join to
form the Truro River—the Allen and the Kenwyn, named after
parishes through which they flow. The original site of the town
was on the ground between the two rivers, sloping steeply up a
hill once dominated by a castle. This disappeared in the reign of
Henry II, its site now occupied by the cattle market, but the
potential for trade at the head of the estuary was a powerful influence for the development of the settlement here. Truro was then,
as it is now, a meeting place of routes, bridges bringing roads
from east and west over the rivers into the town. This medieval
pattern was later superseded as the town grew, and further
bridges were built; now, in the modern fashion, a by-pass takes
through traffic round the town. It was the rise of Falmouth in the
sixteenth century that caused the decline of Truro as a port,
though in addition as the size of ships increased it became more
difficult for them to penetrate so far up the tidal estuary.

Sadly, Truro has been compelled over the years to allow progress to require the destruction of many of its older buildings,
largely for road schemes. The greatest loss was the Red Lion
Hotel, which occupied a prominent site in the main street, a fine
building of the seventeenth century, once kept by the father of
Samuel Foote. This notable figure in the history of the English
stage in the eighteenth century earned a great reputation and no
little notoriety for his satirical sketches, which poked fun or scorn
at individuals or institutions, delighting or infuriating audiences.
The Red Lion faced south across the wide Boscawen Street, still
cobbled; few of the streets in Truro now retain this characteristic,
but the water flowing along the gutters remains an attractive feature. Boscawen Street is dominated by the City Hall, built in 1846
to the Italianate Renaissance design of Christopher Eales.

Truro's main attraction lies in its Georgian heritage, and this is
a reflection of its history: Truro rose to a position of pre-eminence
in Cornwall in the eighteenth century, assuming the unofficial role
of county town which it has retained ever since. The question of

Cornwall's county town has vexed its people for many generations. In medieval times, before communications were opened up,
Launceston held the principal dignity, but this later passed to
Bodmin, which is still officially the county town. However, with
the growth of the population of west Cornwall at the time of the
Industrial Revolution, indeed the concentration of the population
in these parts, Truro became the natural centre for administration. Bodmin remains the assize town, but Truro is the centre of
county government, based on the new County Hall on the
south-western outskirts of the city.

In the eighteenth and early nineteenth century 'the pride of
Truro' became proverbial; it is to the modern city's credit that it
takes proper pride in its architectural heritage from the period.
Lemon Street is the finest Georgian street in the county, the
Orange Street of Hugh Walpole's Polchester, which is based on
Truro. Princes Street contains some stately houses of the gentry,
while at High Cross, the ancient centre of the town, the façade of
the Assembly Rooms is preserved, though the interior has unfortunately not survived. We can only mention a few of the other notable
buildings: the delightful colour-washed range of Strangways
Terrace, the quiet charm of Walsingham Place, the elegance of
the early nineteenth-century Parade. The County Museum of the
Royal Institution of Cornwall in River Street provides an excellent
centre to study Cornish life and history, from prehistoric times to
our own day. Among its exhibits it houses art galleries, a fine
display of natural history and an outstanding collection of minerals. The Royal Institution of Cornwall was founded in 1818; a few
years later in 1835 the granite column at the top of Lemon Street
was built, with its statue by Nevill Northey Burnard commemorating Richard Lander, the Truro-born explorer of the
River Niger.

Born in February 1804 Richard Lander had a short but
remarkable career. His first taste of foreign travel came at the age
of 13 when he went to the West Indies in the care of a merchant.
Africa was to be his chief interest and in 1824 he accompanied the
explorer Clapperton on his expedition to West Africa. Clapperton
died in 1827, whereupon Lander made his way to the coast,
arrived home and published an account of the expedition and his
own travels. This captured attention. An expedition was mounted,
prompted by Lord Bathurst, to explore the Niger, and, accompanied by his younger brother John, Richard Lander arrived in

Africa in February 1830. Five months later the expedition reached the great river, and after an initial exploration up-river turned downstream in order to discover the course of the river, which at that time was unknown. The party were attacked by natives, and then captured; having been eventually ransomed, they reached the delta, and in July 1831 returned home.

The name of Lander was now well known: he published an account of the expedition, and became the first gold medallist of the newly-formed Royal Geographical Society of London. It was not long before some Liverpool merchants realized the possibilities of establishing trade contacts with the region of the Niger and another expedition was organized, with two steamers. After setbacks the boats eventually ascended the river. Having returned to Fernando Po to collect more goods for barter, Lander was rejoining the expedition when he was attacked and received a musket-ball in the thigh. He was taken back to Fernando Po and, despite his iron constitution, died of the wound. There the explorer was buried, but his statue broods over the city where he was born.

From his vantage point Lander surveys the town over the pretty little cupola of St John's Church, built in the late 1820's. There are several churches in Truro, ranging from the quiet dignity of the early nineteenth-century Quaker Meeting House to the up-to-date style of the Roman Catholic church of Our Lady of the Portal and St Piran. Visually the honey-coloured stone front of St Mary's Methodist church is well-proportioned, with the dignity of its age, while unforgettably beautiful is the sound of Kenwyn bells heard in the distance on a quiet evening.

In 1877 Truro acquired the status of a city. Ever since the amalgamation of the sees of St Germans and Crediton and the subsequent creation of the Bishopric of Exeter in 1050, Cornwall was simply an archdeaconry in the vast diocese administered from Exeter. We can imagine how remote the western parts of the county were under medieval conditions of communications. The enormous area needed subdivision, and Truro was the obvious centre of a Cornish diocese. A bishop was appointed, Edward White Benson, a man of remarkable vision and enthusiasm, under whose leadership Cornish churchmen embarked on the project of building a new cathedral. Not since Wren's rebuilding of St Paul's had a cathedral been built in England: here was a real challenge. Within six years Benson himself had left to become Archbishop of

Canterbury, but by then the work was well under way.

Designed by J. L. Pearson, a really distinguished architect, the cathedral is a triumph of Victorian Gothic architecture, conceived basically in the Early English style of the thirteenth century, with great emphasis on the vertical lines. Like all the great Victorian architects, Pearson was a scholar, and a man of his age—a time which saw Early English as the height of architecture, the style fitting for a great building. He seems to have been inspired by Quimper, and it has often been noticed that the style is reminiscent of northern France, which is appropriate considering the historic links between Cornwall and Brittany.

Various sites were considered on the outskirts of the city, but rejected in favour of the central position at High Cross: this was an imaginative choice, and thoroughly justified. Part of the parish church of St Mary was removed to make way, but Pearson retained the richly decorated south aisle and incorporated it into the new building with great skill to continue to serve a parochial function. The most remarkable views of the cathedral are from the east: it rises like granite cliffs above the river at the heart of the city, its towers and pinnacles riding high above the roofs, with the central spire pointing 250 feet into the windy Cornish sky.

Many of the building materials are Cornish, including granite for the walls, and local stone such as polyphant and serpentine. As regards the internal furnishings, an opportunity was perhaps missed in not calling in Sir Ninian Comper. On the other hand, the windows contain fine modern stained glass by Clayton and Bell. Not only the large rose windows in the transepts and the great east and west windows but all the aisle windows follow a carefully prepared sequence. The plan represents the hand of God in history, from the creation and the patriarchs to modern times; it is well worth walking round the building, armed with binoculars, to study the windows as a series. As we walk around the aisles, the pattern of arches and vaulting continually changed. Add to this the Father Willis organ—his last major work—and the building comes to life; triforium and clerestory, transepts and sanctuary, the vaulting of the great central tower, all echo the grandeur of the majestic reeds. Cornish people are rightly proud of their Cathedral, for it was by the gifts and efforts of Cornish people that it was made possible; the recent addition of a chapter house has increased its facilities and scope, and extended its function as the centre of the diocese.

Resuming our journey around the estuary of the Fal we take the road for Falmouth, bringing us first to the parish of Kea, which consists of the residential suburb of Playing Place, the wooded estate of Killiow and the agricultural land running down to the west bank of the river. Old Kea church, of which only a gaunt ruined tower now survives, is hidden away in a secluded corner of the parish by a remote creek; its more accessible late nineteenth-century successor makes one of a triangular group of spires with Baldhu and Devoran, Pearson's other Cornish church.

The neighbouring village of Feock has an attractive situation at the head of Carrick Roads, and as a result there is a good deal of residential development. Two buildings in the area deserve notice, and they could hardly afford a greater contrast. The first is the Quaker Meeting House at the delightfully named hamlet of Come-to-Good, dating from 1709. This is a whitewashed and thatched chapel of great charm, sincere and unpretentious, simply furnished and regularly used. Come-to-Good now lies away from the main roads, but in fact on the old route leading west from King Harry passage, two miles away, and here—in striking contrast to the Quaker Meeting House—the classical and columned Georgian façade of Trelissick House looks down over an undulating park which runs down to the river, commanding a fine view of the estuary. Sheltered behind the house are magnificent gardens, now in the care of the National Trust, where one can stroll along the beech walks to the woods by the water's edge, admire the changing views and discover secret dells full of rare and splendid flowers.

Beyond Feock the road comes to an end at Restronguet Point which marks the end of Restronguet Creek, running up to the former port of Devoran. There is little evidence now of the railway which used to connect the mining areas up the river valley with Devoran, which is now a quiet village lying just off the main road from Truro to Falmouth. This road accompanies one arm of the creek to Perranarworthal where the inn is a reminder of the former timber trade with Norway. Another monument to the past here at Perran Wharf is the foundry which was active from the mid-eighteenth century producing engines for the nearby mining district.

The main road hurries on its way towards Penryn and Falmouth, while side roads climb the wooded hills to the parish of Mylor, passing the estate of Carclew; only a fragment now

remains of the beautiful house largely destroyed by fire in 1934.
Here lived William Lemon who made his fortune from mining
and whose family stamped their name and that of their estate on
the southern part of Truro, which they laid out in the early
nineteenth century. The main centre of population in the parish is
at Mylor Bridge, an attractive village at the head of its creek.
Where this creek opens out into the main estuary is the churchtown of Mylor; the church preserves a fair amount of Norman
building and some good original work in the rood screen, while
the churchyard contains the tallest of the old Cornish crosses, and
a detached bell tower. It occupies a wonderful setting looking
across to St Just on the opposite shore, over a mile away across
the open waters where the yachts scud in the stiffening breezes or
idle in the warmth of summer afternoons.

The ancient town of Penryn has a distinctively Regency style
and would be attractive if traffic from Falmouth were not forced
to pass through it. The clock tower of the Town Hall dominates
the skyline, and there are houses of style and character, many of
them built of local granite. With the growth of Falmouth and the
silting up of the river Penryn declined in importance, but in the
Middle Ages it was a thriving community. The Bishops of Exeter
first developed the place in the early thirteenth century and it
became an important market centre. Its position near the mouth
of the estuary gave it an advantage over Truro as a port but at the
same time there was always the danger of attack by raiders.

In the Middle Ages the chief feature of Penryn was Glasney College, founded as a college of secular canons in 1265. It became a
centre of learning with more than a local reputation, though it
was also responsible for literature in the Cornish language, notably the mystery plays. However, with the Reformation all this
came to an end; the community was dispersed, the buildings were
despoiled and sold, and now hardly a trace remains. Meanwhile
the trade of Penryn grew, with ships calling in for provisions,
merchants making use of the markets, and a variety of goods
being handled. The mining industry gave an additional boost to
trade, and another flourishing commodity was granite from the
many quarries in this part of Cornwall. Stone was sent from Penryn for bridges in London and constructional work in many parts
of the world. No longer do large vessels sail up the creek as in the
former days, but boat-building yards thrive beside the water and
the main road runs by its side towards Falmouth.

The town of Falmouth is a comparative newcomer, though the name existed in earlier times, referring to the estuary as a whole, in which Carew said that a hundred vessels might anchor 'and not one see the mast of another'. The estuary has always been a wonderful natural harbour, but no town existed at the westerly extremity apart from a small fishing village. The building of the castles at Pendennis and St Mawes altered the situation, but the creation of Falmouth was only achieved in the face of opposition from Truro and Penryn, whose trade was naturally threatened by a port nearer the mouth of the estuary.

It was the Killigrew family who took the initiative. Sir John Killigrew, part of whose house, Arwennack, survives near the harbour, pushed forward the scheme for developing the site, and gradually quays and inns were built, together with a customs house. Then came the Civil War and the siege of Pendennis, culminating in its eventual surrender. The town continued to grow, and partly thanks to the Killigrews' support of Charles II the town received its charter early in his reign; the church was built (originally Charles church but after the Restoration known as Charles the Martyr) and the future of the town was assured. Though the town now possesses several churches, the ancient mother church lies quietly outside the town at Budock, and there the Killigrews are commemorated in stone and brass.

From a small village Falmouth has developed dramatically, and taken advantage of its situation facing northward to sheltered water and south towards the open sea to play several roles. In early days its trade was very much like that of its neighbour and rival, Penryn, but in 1688 came a significant development: the port became a Post Office Packet Station, becoming the leading Packet Station until the middle of the nineteenth century when Southampton took over. Atlantic storms were not the only hazard to the mail service. Privateers were a constant threat, and in times of war the packet boats ran the gauntlet on every voyage, frequently engaing in hostilities. Add to this the smuggling activities which were a side-line and we can see that life in the packet service was rarely dull.

Fishing was also an important part of the life of the port, but trade declined when Southampton took over the role as the chief Packet Station. But now in 1863 the railway reached Falmouth, a branch line from Truro, and docks were constructed, extending to the deeper waters at the entrance to the harbour. At first ship-building was an important concern; this later declined but Falmouth remains one of the chief repair ports in the country.

Castle Drive, climbing the hill behind the docks, was laid out in 1865, a scenic route around the headland to Pendennis, encircling the castle. For the railway which came with the building of the docks also brought a boost to the growing tourist trade, and another of Falmouth's roles developed. The tourist resort centred itself on the southward-facing coast, and the family hotels rose in great style along the cliff-top above the beaches, so that the holiday industry is now a major part of the town's economy. The town has a variety of attractions for the tourist—the sea and beaches, the narrow streets of the town and the harbour area, gardens with sub-tropical plants, interesting buildings such as the Customs House dating from around 1820, and Pendennis Castle crowning the headland. From this vantage point we can see it all laid out: to one side the harbour and docks and to the other the holiday resort, with the main Gyllingvase Beach and the neighbouring Swanpool Beach, and Maen Porth a mile further on around Pennance Point. To the north and east the great estuary stretches away inland, and to the south-west the succession of headlands carries the eye on past the Helford River to the Lizard peninsula: all told, as fine a succession of views as any in the kingdom.

SEVEN

Industrial Revolution Country

The section of Cornwall's spine from Truro westwards to Hayle is impossible to understand without some idea of the course and extent of Cornish mining. Not that the activity is limited to this one part of the county: we have already encountered evidences of it in east Cornwall, and in fact it is only the north-east of the county that has not been involved in the story. But here in the area around Redruth and Camborne is the heart of the Cornish mining scene, and the industry has left an indelible mark on the landscape.

Cornish mining is chiefly concerned with tin and copper, though various other minerals have been mined at times, including silver, lead, wolfram, tungsten and uranium. Copper mining came into its own in the eighteenth century, but tin was a thriving trade well before the Christian era. The ancients said that the tin trade from Cornwall came from an island named Ictis, almost certainly St Michael's Mount. The tin which the Cornish smelted and brought overland to trade with the merchants was not, however, the result of mining. At this period, and for several centuries to come, it was the product of 'streaming', the working of alluvial deposits; this took place extensively throughout the county, notably on the uplands such as Bodmin Moor and Hensbarrow Downs, and indeed still goes on in a few isolated places. The process involved washing the material dug out, often diverting a stream for the purpose. This practice gradually assisted the natural process of silting up the rivers so that former ports found themselves inaccessible to seagoing boats. Originally tinners did their own smelting, to separate 'white tin' from 'black tin', that is, the metal from the ore; however, this eventually became a specialist affair, the tinners bringing their ore to the more powerful 'blowing-houses'.

At the end of the twelfth century we hear of the tinners as a special class, with a peculiar type of independence. They had the right of 'bounding'—staking their claim and working that piece of land for tin, subject only to a toll paid to the lord of the manor. Moreover they had their own organization, with their own courts and taxation, presided over by the Warden of the Stannaries. There were four stannaries, or areas of tin working: Foweymoor (the present Bodmin Moor), Blackmoor (the now ironic name for Hensbarrow Downs), Tywarnhayle (Carn Brea and the country to the north) and the western district under the combined names of Penwith and Kerrier. Each of these stannaries had its own courts for settling the affairs of tinners, and also its 'coinage' town; these have varied occasionally, but usually consisted of Liskeard, Lostwithiel, Truro and Helston. The term 'coinage' has nothing to do with minting coins, but refers to the practice of assessing the quality of smelted tin by cutting a corner of each block.

By the fifteenth century a decline had set in owing to the inevitable exhaustion of supplies of tin for streaming, and since the tin lodes were underground, mining was obviously the next step. As mines grew deeper, the drainage of water became a chief problem. The earliest systems of pumping were worked by hand, and then horse power was employed, also being applied to raising the ore together with the waste material from the mines. Early in the eighteenth century Newcomen's engine was introduced, which was satisfactory to a depth of 500 feet. As the demand for more powerful machines arose, so the Boulton and Watt engines doubled the depth of operation. The work of such local engineers as Trevithick and Hornblower improved upon the existing machines, and so evolved the Cornish beam engine, which became the standard equipment of the Cornish mine. These engines were housed in solid buildings of granite and slate. Several other buildings clustered around the surface of a mine: sheds for the preparation of the ore, smith's shop, stores, and the count house which acted as the mine office. In addition the burrows of waste material grew as part of the scene, but it is chiefly the engine-houses which have survived the years and, though now roofless, are such a characteristic feature of the Cornish landscape.

It was not until the eighteenth century that the value of the copper lodes was realised, and the exploitation of these resources gave a tremendous boost to Cornish mining. As the trade flourished, so grew the need for adequate transport to convey the ore to the coast. The trails of pack-animals could no longer cope with the quantity produced, and in the early nineteenth century a series of mineral railways came into being, such as that leading to Portreath on the north coast and the Redruth and Chasewater Railway which connected with the port of Devoran on the Fal.

In its heyday copper mining became Cornwall's major industry and the county reigned supreme as the world's principal supplier, at one period producing more than half the world's total output. Then in the mid-nineteenth century other deposits were discovered in Australia and on the American continent. The Cornish industry suffered a severe recession, though at some mines it was discovered that beneath the copper lodes there were supplies of tin, and so shafts were extended and the mines acquired a new lease of life as tin producers.

The early 1870's were boom years for Cornish tin, but later foreign competition again hit Cornish trade hard, and gradually the mines were forced to close; shiploads of emigrants—people who had never before left their county—sought a new life in America, Australia or South Africa. Close-knit Cornish communities grew up in the new mineral areas, where the Cornish names bear witness to their origin, and it was said that wherever in the world there was a hole dug for minerals, there would be a Cornishman at the bottom of it.

In the great days of Cornish mining, there were fortunes to be made for the owners of the land—the mineral lords—and for those astute enough to take their opportunities. Furthermore, in the days of prosperity the mines afforded employment to thousands, with whole families being engaged in the work, women and girls ('bal maidens') on the surface, men and boys below ground. But for the miner the work was arduous and conditions of life offered little compensation. Sometimes wages were so low that riots broke out, as at Truro in 1789 and Redruth in 1796.

The day's work often began and ended with a walk in all weathers between the miner's cottage and the mine itself. The womenfolk and younger boys worked on the ore in the sheds, while the men and boys over ten changed into their underground clothes and prepared for the descent. This involved a climb down ladders, the only light coming from the candles fixed to their hats with clay, to begin the 'core', or shift, which varied in length depending on the heat and ventilation. The atmosphere encouraged chest diseases, and most miners aged prematurely. The work itself was exhausting, and often dangerous with the risks of blasting accidents and collapses of rock or flooding. At the end of the shift came the grim climb up perpendicular ladders to the surface; many shafts were 1,000 feet deep and more, so that for an exhausted man the climb itself was a dangerous business, with frequent accidents. But for the Cornish miners this was their life; they may have had little choice, but it was what they understood.

Gradually the mines were forced to close until only two—South Crofty at Camborne and Geevor in the far west at Pendeen—were still working, keeping the industry alive. It remains to be seen whether the work at Wheal Jane and Mount Wellington mines near Baldhu, west of Truro, will lead to a resurgence of mining on a large scale in Cornwall. However, just as the visitor to Cornwall must be immensely struck by the china clay activity in the centre of the county, so the relics of the great mining days must also catch his eye. So many names in this middle western part of Cornwall contain the word 'wheal', the Cornish word for a mine, and there is hardly a vantage point in the whole area without a view of several of the abandoned workings, 'knackt bals' in the Cornish language.

An overall picture of this area of Cornwall can be obtained by a climb to the top of Carn Brea, the hill between Camborne and Redruth. The southerly aspect is a scene of granite uplands, thick with clusters of mine workings, chiefly the remains of the Basset mines of Carnkie. But what really takes the eye is the panorama to the north and west. At our feet is the central spine of communication lines, with the railway cutting its way west from Redruth to Camborne and on, eventually to Penzance; beyond it the A30 trunk road winds its way through the built-up areas, much of the new development covering the sites of former mining activity. Beyond this again is the latest highway, the modern dual carriageway taking traffic north of the industrial area, sweeping the road over graceful bridges which span the valleys leading down to the coast. Westward from St Agnes Beacon, the hill to the north-east, the land between the industrial strip and the coast is mainly a plateau, with little variation apart from valleys and inlets such as Portreath straight ahead of us. Away to the west the cliffs of the north coast give way to the sandy towans north of Hayle, where the river opens out into a broad estuary; beyond this again rise the heights of Penwith.

As we travel along the road west from Truro, so we find a marked change in the landscape. Leaving behind the built-up area we pass through agricultural country until we reach the descent to the village of Chacewater, when the signs of mining appear. Chacewater itself is a mining village, with a number of small houses of Georgian and early Victorian vintage, the years of mining prosperity. The tall, narrow church tower standing sternly on its hillside almost seems to reflect the empty shells of the engine-houses which dominate the district. The main railway line passes to the north of the village, and a branch line to Perranporth and Newquay was opened in 1903, but was axed after 60 years. The course of the line, now bereft of rails, still winds its way towards the coast over viaducts and through deserted cuttings gradually being claimed by undergrowth.

The road to the west now passes a number of engine-houses associated with Wheal Busy, one of the oldest copper mines and very productive in its day. In the late 1770's James Watt, who was based with his partner Matthew Boulton at Birmingham, was staying at Chacewater while the first of his pumping engines was being installed at this mine, but there were always strained relations between the Scotsman and the Cornish engineers.

As we continue westwards, we see on our left the woods of Scorrier House. It was in the eighteenth century that the Williams family became established as one of the foremost in west Cornwall, their foundation firmly laid on mineral wealth. They were a family of great imagination and industry. John Williams was manager of Poldice mine, which was owned by William Lemon of Carclew—another whose rapid rise was entirely due to a fortune won from mining. One of Williams' important achievements was the Great County Adit, a vast and intricate drainage system. It took 20 years to drive the tunnels from the outfall near Bissoe, in the valley above Devoran, but eventually the network was draining about 50 mines in the area south of Chacewater and almost as far as Redruth, a tremendous achievement. This family eventually took over Caerhays Castle from the Trevanions, but on their own ground at Scorrier they laid the Poldice to Portreath tramroad as a means of linking the mining area with the coast.

At Scorrier the road from Truro joins the A30 trunk road, and together they advance towards Redruth, the old capital of the

Mining Division. As Redruth and her neighbour Camborne have grown towards each other, they have become known as the urban district of Camborne-Redruth, which tends to obscure the seniority of the eastern partner, a town of some character. Much of the commercial part of the town has been standardized with modern shop fronts, but there is still plenty of good Georgian and early Victorian building. The main street climbs up either side of a valley, the eastern part passing an Italianate clock-tower on its way up to the fine rectangular Wesleyan chapel of 1826.

The railway crosses the southern part of the town on a viaduct, and the road to Falmouth emerges from below it to set out along the valley between the two hills of Carn Brea and Carn Marth. A couple of miles along the road is the village of Lanner, very much a mining settlement, with its cottages and chapels, serving the copper mining area in the hillside above the village. Pre-eminent among these mines was Tresavean, one of the deepest and most productive in Cornwall. It has a place in history partly because of its depth, since in 1842 there was installed here the first engine to carry men up and down the shaft and save them the laborious and dangerous climb up ladders to the surface. Half a century earlier Redruth had witnessed another innovation when William Murdoch, working for the firm of Boulton and Watt, and himself a Scotsman, for the first time lit his house and office with gas.

We resume our journey west from Redruth, with continuous building along either side of the road, overlooked on the south by the brooding bulk of Carn Brea. Illogan Highway merges into Pool in a nondescript urban sprawl, with little to tempt the visitor to stop and explore. Yet anyone whose interest in Cornish mining is aroused by the recurring reminders of this once great industry will find here at Pool a close link with the days when the extraction of minerals was the area's principal activity. East Pool mine was a notable example of a copper mine which, when deposits appeared to be exhausted, went deeper and acquired a new lease of life as a tin producer. Its great days were in the nineteenth century, but it was working as late as the end of the Second World War, when production finally ceased.

The significance of East Pool mine today is that here are preserved two beam engines, both of which were actually in use for many years. These engines were saved when the mine closed down, and were presented to the Cornish Engines Preservation Society; they are now in the care of the National Trust, which maintains them in good order. One does not have to be an engineer to be impressed with their size and power. When we look at a ruined engine-house standing in isolation on a cliff-top or amongst a waste of spoil heaps it is difficult to imagine it as a scene of activity or indeed to picture its appearance when housing an engine; a visit to East Pool brings the scene to life.

Beside the main road stands a steam 'whim' or winding engine for conveying ore and men up a shaft. The engine consists chiefly of a rocking beam whose up-and-down motion is converted to rotary action by means of a crank on the drum shaft. Inside the engine-house the bottom chamber is dominated by the cylinder and the controls for the driver; the top of the cylinder, which has a diameter of 30 inches, can be seen from the middle chamber, and here we can appreciate the nine-foot stroke of the piston attached to the inner end of the 'bob', as the beam is known in Cornwall. Climbing to the top chamber we are alongside the bob itself, the centre of which is secured on the massively constructed bob wall, one of the four outside walls of the engine-house. Seventeen times a minute the piston rocks the bob in its bearings, and outside the house its outer end maintains the regular rotation of the drums.

Years of experience resulted in engines of this type, remarkably efficient and economical to work; this engine was in fact the last rotative beam engine made in Cornwall, manufactured in Camborne in 1887. Not far from the winding engine is another and larger engine, this one employed for pumping water from the mine. It was working until 1954, pumping water from a depth of 1,700 feet. The interior of this engine-house is similar to the other but on a grander scale—this cylinder has a diameter of 90 inches, and ran at a speed of about five or six strokes a minute, each stroke moving a weight of about 84 tons of water in the shaft. The size of the machine is colossal, the huge bob weighing 52 tons. The smaller winding engine is in working order so that we can observe the operation of the piston, the rocking bob and the rotating drums, but the pumping engine is now motionless, like a sleeping giant. The visitor cannot fail to be impressed, or to feel respect for the engineers who produced these powerful machines in the days when hundreds of engines were continually at work throughout Cornwall.

The most famous name in Cornish engineering is that of Richard Trevithick, born not far from here in 1771. His father was a respected figure in the mining world, and the son, a handsome young giant, began to make a name for himself because of his feats of strength and daring. He was also earning a reputation as an engineer, and applied his mind to the improvement of engines by the use of high-pressure steam, not without incurring the opposition of Watt, whose machines worked on the low-pressure principle. From stationary engines Trevithick's mind turned to the design and construction of a locomotive worked by steam power. After various experiments a full-size machine was built in Camborne, and at the end of 1801 'Captain Dick' took his road-locomotive for its run between Camborne and Tehidy, to the amazement—and apprehension—of the local people. The event is remembered to this day in the folk lines sung at popular occasions:

> Goin' up Camborne 'ill, Comin' down,
> Goin' up Camborne 'ill, Comin' down,
> The 'osses stood still, the wheels turned aroun',
> Goin' up Camborne 'ill, Comin' down.

The next demonstration took place in London, after which came the development of putting the locomotive on rails and attaching wagons to it: this took place in South Wales. Then after a few years, including a visit by Trevithick to the north of England to meet George Stephenson, London saw the railway in the shape of a circular track at Euston where passengers paid to travel by the novel means of transport. However, after an accident put paid to the Euston 'catch me who can' demonstration, it was typical of Trevithick that he abandoned work on locomotives, leaving others to continue the work he had pioneered, while he turned his attention to other applications of high-pressure steam, including a steam threshing-machine.

His restless spirit took him in 1816 to South America to supervise the installation of machinery at the gold and silver mines of Peru. All seemed set fair on this enterprise when the country was suddenly plunged into revolution. After serving in Bolivar's army he set off for Costa Rica and almost perished in the jaws of an alligator. Penniless as he was at this time, he met—of all people—Robert Stephenson, who gave him the cash for the voyage to England. He returned home to the welcoming sound of Camborne church bells, his days of excitement over. He continued to devote himself to engineering inventions, but his health declined and in 1833 while working at a factory at Dartford he died, penniless and away from his family and friends. His statue in Camborne, depicting him holding a model of his locomotive, is a constant reminder to Cornish people of this remarkable genius.

Another benefactor of mining, not only in Cornwall, lived at Tuckingmill, the next link in the urban chain before we reach Camborne. This was William Bickford, whose invention of the safety-fuse undoubtedly saved many lives, since previously blasting had been a far more risky affair. Bickford established a factory here in 1830 which produced fuse at an increasing rate until its closure in 1961, when it turned to the making of agricultural machinery.

A stream flows north from Nine Maidens Down on the shoulder of Carnmenellis and passes through Tuckingmill on its way to join the other stream making up the Red River, reaching the sea at the eastern end of St Ives Bay. The existence of the stream accounts for the name Tuckingmill—the word used in Cornwall and Devon for a fulling mill, where the last stage in the process of making cloth took place, the material being dipped, scoured and beaten. Charles Henderson noted the sites of almost 60 of these mills in the county, several still preserving the name Tuckingmill or the Cornish word 'Velyn-druckya'.

Pressing on westward up the hill from the stream we reach Camborne at the western end of the industrial belt. At the great Dolcoath mine here the lowest levels were at a depth of over 3,000 feet—twelve times the height of Truro Cathedral spire. The town owes its development almost entirely to the mining boom, but the village from which it grew was served by the parish church, a fifteenth-century granite building, now with an extra south aisle added in 1878. There are monuments to the Pendarves family, who lived at their grand house in its estate south of the town; the house itself was demolished in 1955, leaving its early Victorian chapel and the somewhat melancholy Gothic family mausoleum. Mining itself has almost ceased in Camborne, but the engineering firm of Holman has been established here since 1839, producing mining machinery throughout the latter years of the industry; and in another sense the town is still the mining centre, since here is the School of Mines, the only metalliferous mining school in the country, attracting students from all over the world.

In 1931 traces of a Roman villa were discovered at Magor, north of Camborne, where the land slopes gradually westwards towards the Red River. The site, the most westerly Roman villa yet known, was excavated and studied, though not maintained as

an ancient monument. It was grand by comparison with neighbouring dwellings, though not by Roman standards, being probably built by a successful Cornishman who had returned home
after experiencing the benefits of Roman life in the east of the
province. Its corridor and pavement, together with its half a
dozen or so rooms, must have impressed the locals, who were not
to know the grander villas of which this was an amateurish copy.
Together with the camps at Nanstallon and Carvosso, Magor is
significant in its indication that there was a greater Roman presence in Cornwall than used to be thought.

The spinal road heads away to the west, towards Hayle and the
granite peninsula of Penwith. A long hill winds down to a branch
of the Red River at the hamlet of Roseworthy. Most traffic, in
either direction, seems in a hurry to rush through the village and
atttack the opposite hill, but to do so is to miss the most attractive
late Georgian chapel, built in a simple and modest style in 1825. As
we reach the top of the hill beyond Roseworthy and pass through
the village of Connor Downs, so a fine view unfolds. The country
slopes away to the estuary of the River Hayle, two miles ahead,
while beyond rise the highlands of Penwith; to our right are the
sand hills behind the eastern arm of St Ives Bay, and beyond the
river the distant coastline curves around to St Ives Head, with the
town itself climbing the hill above its harbour.

Behind the appearance of Hayle there is a great deal more than
is at first evident. A discerning eye can see from the great
warehouses and wharves beside the estuary what a prime part it
played as an Industrial Revolution port. It derives its name from
the Cornish word for an estuary, *heyle*. In the earliest days this
estuary was the northern end of the trade route which linked the
north coast with Mount's Bay; before the silting up of the River
Hayle, navigation was possible as far as St Erth, which meant an
overland journey of only about three miles, greatly preferable to
the perilous voyage around Land's End.

One of the best ways to appreciate the landscape here is to
climb Trencrom Hill, two miles or so to the west. From this vantage point the whole of St Ives Bay can be seen. The river flowing
north opens out into a broad estuary, which presents varying
appearances according to the state of the tide and attracts many
species of birds. The opening to the sea is comparatively narrow,
but this is where the traders came with their cargoes, and sometimes not only traders. In the age of the saints, the travellers from

Wales tended to arrive at the Camel estuary; here further west was the landing place for those sailing from Ireland, whether by boat or, as the legends assure us, by less conventional means of transport, such as millstones, troughs or leaves. It seems that several Irish missionaries or colonists landed here in the 6th century and, despite persecution by the local king, settled at various places in west Cornwall.

The estuary was a valuable port in medieval times, with Lelant on its western bank and Hayle developing on the eastern arm of the inlet until the silting up of the river. The most important growth of Hayle came with the rise of the mining industry in the eighteenth century. The harbour was developed, and a canal constructed beside the estuary. For a time the smelting of copper took place here, until it was found uneconomical to import coal for the purpose, and so the ore was shipped to South Wales for smelting. This phase of Hayle's past is preserved in the name Copperhouse, at the eastern side of the present town.

The major industrial concern at Hayle started during the eighteenth century. From a modest beginning the firm of Harvey's became the leading engineering firm in the county, involved in ship-building and trading, in addition to supplying from the foundry much of the machinery in demand for the mining industry, not only in Cornwall but all over the world. In the 1840's the firm built and installed the largest steam engines in the world to drain the Haarlem Lake in Holland. There was also another foundry established at Copperhouse, and the town flourished; its prosperity is reflected in the Georgian and early Victorian houses which face the estuary. The recession in the mining industry meant an inevitable decline in the fortunes of the port and accounts for the impression of decadence one might experience here. Yet the area attracts the holiday visitors, who throng to the sandy beaches north of the town.

We shall now leave the Hayle area and work our way back to it by way of the north coast. Our last glimpse of that coast was at Perranporth, now a holiday centre but in its time a mining district with one mine actually in what is now the main street. The coast road climbs a steep hill to the high platform which lies behind the cliffs from here to the eastern end of St Ives Bay. This plateau has one notable hill, St Agnes Beacon, and a succession of valleys—'coombes' as they are known in this part of Cornwall—where streams run down to the sea, but is otherwise of a

uniform height, and as a result provided the sites for two airfields.
We pass the first of these on leaving Perranporth; it is now a home
for gliders, which use the currents rising over the cliffs. The cliff
walk from Perranporth to St Agnes is most spectacular, with fine
views along the coast, and the relics of mining operations; this
area was once rich in copper deposits. Beyond the airfield is the
steep valley of Trevellas Coombe. Here in overgrown solitude a
stream bubbles along its rocky bed between increasingly bare hills,
where formerly the Blue Hills tin mine was at work.

We are now moving from copper to tin mining country around
St Agnes, which owes its existence to tin mining, though it is now
an attractive and comparatively unspoilt holiday centre. Trevau-
nance Cove at the foot of the valley was a harbour for the export
of tin in the eighteenth and nineteenth centuries, but it was
always difficult to maintain it against the attacks of the sea, and
the project was eventually abandoned. Up the hill in the churchtown the mine workings are close at hand, the engine-houses
almost peering over the shoulders of the houses.

West of St Agnes is a waste of old tin workings where nature is
reclaiming the ground. The hill of St Agnes Beacon dominates the
landscape with its extensive views of the coast from St Ives to
Trevose Head, a procession of headlands interspersed with rocky
inlets and sandy beaches; inland the view includes a large area of
mid-Cornwall, the bulk of Carn Brea rising to the south and keeping watch over the industrial belt. The Beacon is in the care of the
National Trust, as is a good deal of this north coast, which consequently retains its grandeur.

The coast path passes the ruins of Wheal Coates, perched near
the edge of the cliffs. In the last century the mine supplied both
copper and tin; now its abandoned engine-house supplies material
for the photographer, and adds a touch of melancholy to the
astonishing scenery. The next inlet is Chapel Porth, unspoilt by
buildings thanks to being in the care of the National Trust, like
the cliffs on either side. This is now copper country again, and a
group of mines in the next valley show the extent to which the
area was worked, the land being particularly scarred and arid.
This valley reaches the coast at Porthtowan, a larger inlet than
Chapel Porth with a greater expanse of beach, and consequently
more developed as a holiday resort. The road from Porthtowan
turns away from the coast to avoid the former airfield site of Nan-
cekuke Common and makes for Illogan. Of the fourteenth-century

church here only the tower remains, the present building on a new site dating from 1846 and notable for its monuments to the Basset family.

A bust by Westmacott commemorates the most eminent member of that family, Francis Basset, Lord de Dunstanville, who played a great part in the Industrial Revolution in Cornwall. A member of Parliament for many years, he wrote on politics and agriculture, founded the Royal Cornwall Infirmary in Truro and was a leading figure in the world of Cornish mining, working for the miners' welfare and supporting Trevithick's experiments. In 1836, the year after his death, the obelisk on Carn Brea was set up in his memory, looking across from the wind-swept hill to the woods of Tehidy where he had lived; his home, one of the grand-est of Cornish houses, was destroyed by fire in 1919, and the estate now supports a hospital and a golf course.

It was due to Basset's enterprise that the nearby cove of Por-treath was developed as a harbour to serve the mines of the area, in the same way as the efforts at St Agnes. Whereas the Trevau-nance Cove harbour did not survive the attacks of the sea, Por-treath harbour, tucked in at the eastern end of the beach, proved more permanent and exists now. A pier reaches out to form a narrow entrance, exposed to the force of the north wind and winter storms, leading to the more sheltered inner harbour and quay. The hills rise steeply on either side of the valley leading to the village, and on the west side are the remains of the incline up which cargoes were hauled by a stationary engine at the top, ready for the rail journey to the mines. Some pleasant older houses remain as a reminder of the former activity of the port, together with an increasing growth of holiday residences, the modern industry taking over from the old.

Having climbed the hill west of Portreath we are once more on the high platform, and we can follow the coast road along Reska-jeage Downs towards Gwithian and Hayle or better still walk the coastal footpath. Most of the coastal strip from Portreath to God-revy Point and round to the Red River is National Trust property, and there is no shortage of spectacular cliff scenery, such as Ralph's Cupboard and Hell's Mouth. The names of this inlet and the neighbouring Deadman's Cove are a reminder that this is a distinctly inhospitable shore for shipping, even though in former days men who knew the coast well sometimes used these coves for smuggling operations.

Rounding the headlands of Navax Point and Godrevy Point we come to St Ives Bay, with the famous fishing port itself four miles away at the western end of the bay; the eastern end is guarded by the lighthouse on Godrevy Island which inspired Virginia Woolf's novel *To the Lighthouse*. Beyond this point the cliffs give way to a three-mile stretch of towans or sand dunes, now being colonized by holiday accommodation and caravans but for centuries bare and lonely. Gwithian commemorates one of the Irish arrivals who suffered for their faith, like neighbouring Gwinear, first of the Cornish martyrs. An oratory similar to that of St Piran at Perranzabuloe was built here, not far from the bridge taking the road over the Red River, but a similar fate overtook it when it was claimed by the shifting sands. Traces of earlier occupation have been found on Gwithian Towans, a Bronze Age settlement, though no signs of it are now visible.

The branch railway line to St Ives running beside the estuary joins the main line at St Erth station, which lies close to the main road to Penzance. The village of St Erth is situated about a mile upstream from the end of the estuary, at the head of the tidal reach of the River Hayle, and formerly the height of navigation. When John Leland, Henry VIII's Antiquary, made his tour of Cornwall in 1538 he found the river choked on account of tin working further upstream, though he was informed that it was not very long since ships had been able to sail as far as this point. In his notes he also refers to the bridge carrying the main road to the west, which was then 200 years old; on account of its strategic position and increasing use, repair work and widening were necessary from time to time, but the main burden was removed from it in 1825 when the road beside the estuary was opened to take the bulk of the traffic. The bridge as we see it today is mainly seventeenth-century work.

One of the last operations on the bridge was organized by a celebrated Cornishman, Davies Gilbert of Tredrea. This enterprising and generous man, born here in 1767, was Member of Parliament for Helston and then Bodmin. He was a most able mathematician and statistician, and also a writer on Cornish affairs; his *Parochial History of Cornwall* was published in 1838. However, his interests were not merely local—he was a President of the Royal Society. He was a keen supporter of the work of Trevithick, and actively involved himself in his experiments; he acted as stoker when the great engineer first put his steam engine through its paces at home in Camborne, a year or two before its first startling appearance on the road. It was a notable epoch in Cornish history through which he lived, and to which he contributed, witnessing the beginning of the railway age before his death in 1839.

The 11 mile journey of the River Hayle begins in bare country, though it flows through woods in its lower reaches above St Erth. It rises in the parish of Crowan, which brings us back within sight of the central mining area; the village of Praze-an-Beeble, on the road from Camborne to Helston, grew up as a mining settlement at a crossroads. The rather bare scenery of this district is relieved by the woods of Clowance, an estate through which the infant Hayle runs. The old house was destroyed by fire, and the present house is an early Victorian granite building, rather severe in style with its Tuscan porch.

Clowance was the ancient seat of the St Aubyn family who as leading Parliamentarians acquired St Michael's Mount from the impoverished Bassets during the Commonwealth period. The parish church of Crowan contains family monuments from several centuries, including Sir John St Aubyn, who died in 1772, a benefactor of the tinners and an incorruptible member of Parliament of whom Sir Robert Walpole declared, 'Every man has his price except the little Cornish baronet'. A later member of the family was the architect J. P. St Aubyn, whose appalling bad taste has disfigured many churches throughout the county.

As we continue eastwards, the bulk of Carnmenellis rises ahead, the highest point in this part of Cornwall; near the road a mile to the west are two stone circles. A far more recent addition to the landscape lies on the other side of the hill—Stithians Reservoir, which spreads itself to north and south with several bays and inlets dictated by the lie of the land. The village of Stithians itself lies to the east of the reservoir; to the south of the village are numerous granite quarries near Mabe and Longdowns, eastwards the stream flows through the wooded Kennal Vale to Ponsanooth and eventually out to the Fal, and to the north are the mines of Gwennap.

It used to be said in the great days of Cornish mining that the area north of Gwennap was the richest square mile of ground in the Old World. Certainly the Consolidated Mines in the early nineteenth century were the richest in the world, producing enormous yields of copper. This area with its villages of Gwen-

nap, St Day, Carharrack and Twelveheads supported numerous
mines, many of them drained by the Great Adit with its outlet at
Bissoe and served by the railroads running north to Portreath and
south to Devoran. William Beckford described a visit to these
mines in 1787: 'the consolidated mines . . . are situated in a bleak
desert, rendered still more doleful by the unhealthy appearance of
its inhabitants. At every step one stumbles upon ladders that lead
into utter darkness, or funnels that exhale warm copperous vap-
ours. . . . Huge iron engines creaking and groaning, invented by
Watt, and tall chimneys smoking and flaming, that seem to
belong to old Nicholas' abode, diversifying the prospect'.

Many of the tall chimneys remain, no longer smoking and flaming, but silent, reminders of the former activity in this desolate
region. Gorse, brambles and ivy now claim the engine-houses,
jackdaws fly in the empty sockets of the windows, and all around
are the arid spoil heaps which cover this magnificently melancholy
landscape.

On the east of this district is the parish of Baldhu ('the black
mine'), including the hamlets of Bissoe and Twelveheads and the
renewed tin mining activity at Wheal Jane. The church stands on
the ridge of the hill among pines, its rather squat spire a landmark
from several directions. Three miles away to the south-west, on
the other side of the 'bleak desert', Gwennap churchtown nestles
in a valley, with the woods of Trevince just to the north. The
distinctive feature of the church is the detached bell-tower, with a
conical roof, housing a ring of six bells.

North of Trevince Woods is the village of Carharrack, and
beyond it the straggling capital of this mining world, St Day. The
village has terraces of houses and a granite clock tower in the
centre, surmounted by a wooden bell turret. Medieval pilgrims
came here to the shrine of the Holy Trinity, on their route further
west to St Michael's Mount; the church was built in Georgian
Gothic style in 1828 at the end of the village. On account of its
dangerous condition it has now been closed and stands rather for-
lornly set back from the road. The village sits on the top of a hill,
and from a distance the church tower set about with pinnacles
often catches the eye as one turns a corner.

Most of this area can be seen from the vantage point of Carn
Marth, south-east of Redruth. To the west is the neighbouring hill
of Carn Brea, with a similar view to the north coast beyond the
urban area along the central highway. A large quarry has eaten

into the side of Carn Marth, and on top of the hill a peaceful and mysterious pool now fills an abandoned quarry. To the south and east is an unparalleled view. Stithians Reservoir lies in the shadow of Carnmenellis, and as our gaze turns eastward the sea comes into view, stretching from Falmouth Bay to St Austell Bay, a perfect balance to the north coast view from St Ives to Trevose Head. Inland from the uplifted headland of the Dodman are the white pyramids above St Austell, while far beyond to the north-east Brown Willy and Roughtor rise from the Moor. From here we have sight of most Cornish activities: the industrial area just to the north, the docks at Falmouth, china clay works, north coast beaches gleaming in the sun, farmland with grazing herds, the mine stacks bearing proud and dignified witness to the great days of mineral wealth.

Less than a mile to the north it is possible to see Gwennap Pit, midway between Redruth and St Day. This is a remarkable circular amphitheatre on the lower slopes of the hill, originally a disused mine working. Its grassy sides have now been neatly shaped into 13 tiers, accommodating roughly 2,000 people, and has a notable place in an aspect of Cornish history to which we have as yet made only passing reference—Methodism. But just as visitors to Cornwall can hardly ignore china clay works or disused engine-houses, so they must notice the numbers of chapels which occur in the larger towns and the small hamlets, even in isolated situations in the country districts.

John Wesley was one of the greatest men of his time. The establishment of a church which was not merely a local but a world-wide movement was a tremendous achievement, though it was never his original intention to do other than supplement the work of the Anglican Church. A man of immense energy, he visited Cornwall 32 times between 1743 and 1789 and changed the life of the county by his own preaching and by the organization of which he was the leader and guide. The Church in the eighteenth century was unable to cope with the expansion of the mining parishes, and the needs of the fast-growing numbers of miners were neglected. Cornwall was merely an archdeaconry in the diocese of Exeter, and was rarely visited by either bishop or archdeacon.

It was to visit a religious society at St Ives that the Wesleys first came to Cornwall in 1743, and they had a mixed reception. The difficulties they had to face in the first three years would have

daunted lesser men, but John Wesley's calmness and fearlessness
saw them through. It was unfortunate for them that these first
years coincided with the Jacobite threat which culminated in the
rising of 1745; the magistrates were suspicious of any gathering,
and as the evangelists' preaching caused societies to grow in
numbers, particularly attracting the poorer classes, so official
attitudes hardened against them. They were attacked by angry
mobs, especially at St Ives and Falmouth, as their journals record.
But with the defeat of the Pretender at Culloden, the Jacobite
threat disappeared, and John Wesley recorded what a different
reception they encountered.

During the following years the journeys met with ever-
increasing success, and Methodism became established in the
hearts of the people. Several times Wesley preached at Gwennap
Pit to enthusiastic crowds; his last visit there was on 23 August,
1789, when he estimated the numbers at about 25,000. Five days
later he left Cornwall for the last time, recording in his journal,
'So there is a fair prospect in Cornwall, from Launceston to
Land's End'.

The influence of Wesley's work on the Cornish people cannot
be measured, though it certainly had a great civilizing effect on
the rough miners and gave a new dimension to their lives. What
can be seen, however, is the large number of chapels around the
county, particularly in the mining areas. Originally 'society'
houses were simple in design and construction; Methodists often
attended the parish church regularly, but gradually the links were
broken, and as numbers and resources increased, so more imposing permanent chapels were built. Charles Wesley wrote upward
of 6,000 hymns, and music always played a large part in
Methodism. Hymns would be sung not only in chapels but wherever men felt moved to sing—in their houses or deep in the mines.
Furthermore, in the days of emigration the hymns became part of
the tradition the miners took with them, part of their way of life.

Sometimes we find two chapels quite close to each other, a
reflection of the divisions which came into Methodism as time
went by. Such a group were the Bible Christians, the 'Bryanites',
founded by William Brian (later O'Bryan) from Luxulyan who
started itinerant preaching in north Cornwall. One of the most
famous Bible Christians was Billy Bray, born in 1794 at Twelveheads. This ebullient character was a hard-drinking, dissolute
miner who experienced a conversion after which he became an

enthusiastic preacher who walked for miles to speak at meetings and built chapels with his own hands. Joy radiated from this little man, who was never slow to express his feelings, and who frequently broke into a dance for sheer enthusiasm. He lies buried in the churchyard at Baldhu, not far from the chapels he built and in the parish through which he danced with such exuberance.

Gwennap Pit is now trim and orderly, having been tidied and made smaller since the days of Wesley's visits. It was originally only by chance that he used the Pit for a meeting, being prevented by a high wind from using his normal site for preaching. However, from that beginning sprang a tradition, and an annual gathering still takes place here. While the chapels throughout the length of the county continue the work the Wesleys began and echo to their hymns, it is in places such as this that one can try to capture the spirit of the original preaching missions and appreciate the social revolution which they set in motion. Even if 25,000 was an exaggeration, what fervour must have attended the preaching of the indomitable little man who so deeply impressed the Cornish people 200 years ago.

EIGHT

The Southern Peninsula

From our vantage point at Pendennis Castle we could see the coastline leading the eye away over Falmouth Bay to the south and west. The typical Cornish pattern of headlands and beaches is broken by the larger inlet where the Helford River opens to the sea, and as the coast turns away west out of our vision the waves continually break over the Manacles. Inland from these dangerous rocks the spire of St Keverne church pricks the skyline, and the land is a pattern of hills and woods. Over the horizon is a different world, the plateau of the Lizard peninsula, which is unlike any other part of Cornwall; this eastern arm of Mount's Bay brings us round to Helston, the capital of this southern extremity of the county, and so to another mining district. All told, this area which we are now to consider is one of great contrast and variety.

From the parish of Budock we move into Mawnan, a beautiful coastal district on the north side of the Helford estuary. The Helford River is not long, but its drowned valley gives it a broad estuary with a number of creeks on either bank. The National Trust protects Rosemullion Head, which forms the southern end of Falmouth Bay, and the northern shore at the mouth of the Helford comprising Toll Point and Parson's Beach. As one might suppose, immediately above Parson's Beach is Mawnan church, at the end of a lane in one corner of the parish; the view from the porch is breath-taking. A path from the churchyard leads down towards the water, and the coast commands the view across to the southern shore and also for two miles or so up the river; woods reach to the water's edge and small boats move here and there or ride quietly at anchor. Also in the care of the National Trust is the garden of Glendurgan, a luxuriant wooded valley full of rare shrubs, running down to the hamlet of Durgan by the water's edge.

Less than a mile up-river from Durgan is the ferry crossing linking Helford Passage with the village of Helford on the southern shore. This ancient ferry was formerly in the control of the Bishops of Exeter, who owned a manor south of the river. They also had jurisdiction over fishing and oyster beds between this point and the sea. The flourishing oyster concern is now controlled by the Duchy of Cornwall Oyster Farm with its centre at Porth Navas, on the creek just up-river again from the ferry.

The road around the head of the creek is typical of this area, narrow and winding, with hills and sharp corners; the views of the water here are idyllic, and the village of Porth Navas delightful. We are now in the parish of Constantine, and the road makes for the churchtown, with a lane leading to Calamansack and the woods beside the river. In this area one cannot help thinking of Q's wonderful evocation of *Helford River:*

> *Helford River, Helford River,*
> *Blessed may ye be!*
> *We sailed up Helford River*
> *By Durgan from the sea.*

> *All the wood to ransack,*
> *All the wave explore—*
> *Moon on Calamansack,*
> *Ripple on the shore.*

The next creek has two arms reaching up to Polpenwith and Polwheveral, and on the high ground between the streams feeding the creek is the village of Constantine. For this district it is a substantial village; there are quarries in the north of the parish, which provided granite for the church. In the church is a brass of 1574 which is a palimpsest on the reverse of a fourteenth-century Flemish knight. The exterior retains its grandeur and stands up well in its commanding situation.

North of the village is the interesting house of Trewardreva, an early seventeenth-century E-shaped manor house, with an exceedingly fine Queen Anne wing looking down the valley. Not far away is a relic of earlier occupation, Trewardreva Fogou, sometimes known as Piskey's Hall. Fogous—the word derives from the

Cornish *ogo*, a cave—were associated with fortified sites, and consisted of an underground passage, walled and roofed with stone, slightly curved, 50 or 60 feet long and approximately the height of a man. They are found more in west Cornwall than in other parts, but their purpose is not firmly established: they may have been designed for storage, or for defence, or for prehistoric ritual purposes.

The old port of Gweek lies at the head of the estuary, now little more than a village on the road between Helston and Penryn, but formerly a centre of activity at the quayside. When in the fourteenth century Helston was denied access to the west coast, as we shall see later, Gweek became the leading port of the area. Not that its history began at this period, since various tracks converged here during previous centuries, but the increased activity in the mining district near Wendron made it busier; the produce of the mines was brought here, and timber from Scandinavia was imported for use in the mines.

From this meeting place of roads we take the route for St Keverne, which runs through woods and enters the district south of the river known as Meneage. Here is the parish of Mawgan is Trelowarren, the home of the Vyvyan family. This charming, low two-storey building is a fascinating composition, because of the different dates of its construction; mainly an early seventeenth-century building, it has the rarity of a Georgian Gothic chapel. The extensive estate includes Halligye Fogou, the largest of these constructions in Cornwall, extending 90 feet.

Pressing on westwards, back towards the coast, we pass through St Martin-in-Meneage and cross the stream leading down to the well-known Frenchman's Creek, where the trees overhang the water's edge. From the next village of Manaccan one road runs down to the yachtsman's village of Helford and another leads to the headland at the entrance to the estuary, looking across to Mawnan where our tour round the river began. The Cornish *dinas* occurs again here, the promontory being Dennis Head and the blockhouse (fortified by the Royalists in the Civil War) Little Dennis. The road ends at the attractive St Anthony-in-Meneage, which faces the village of Gillan across the creek. There is little at St Anthony except for the church by the shore, but this in itself makes a visit worthwhile; it was sensitively restored and retains old woodwork in the roof and a splendid set of brass candelabra. This, added to its marvellous setting near the water, makes St

Anthony one of the gems of an area of great beauty.

St Keverne is the largest and most varied parish in Meneage. In the centre of the village is a square, with the church at one side of it. Its tall tower and spire make a distinctive landmark; the spire is visible from the sea, and for that reason was immediately rebuilt when struck by lightning in 1770. The coast here is notorious for shipwrecks when south-easterly winds have driven vessels on to the neighbouring rocks, the Manacles (*maen eglos*—church stone). One of the worst disasters was the wreck of the *Mohegan* in 1898; the chancel window commemorates the dead who lie buried in the churchyard.

Historically St Keverne made a reputation for producing leaders of revolt. The first occasion was in 1497 when the blacksmith Michael Joseph led a protest against a tax levied to pay for a distant war against the Scots. They acquired a spokesman in Thomas Flamank, a Bodmin lawyer, and marched to London; the royal forces, however, routed the Cornishmen, and the leaders ended their days at Tyburn.

Half a century later a priest of St Keverne, Martin Geoffrey, took the lead in resisting the reforming activities of William Body in Helston. Body was enforcing the orders forbidding images, candles and other Popish hindrances to worship, and was attacked and killed by the angry mob. This outburst came to nothing, and Geoffrey and the other leaders suffered the fate of Joseph and Flamank, but it was the forerunner of worse trouble. The year 1549 saw the Prayer Book Rebellion, when westcountrymen rose in protest against the English Prayer Book. The Cornish in particular objected to having services in a foreign language—English—though they could hardly have understood the traditional Latin, and it was their innate conservatism and the leadership of their priests that inspired them. This rebellion was a more serious affair, but after some months authority triumphed, and the Cornish had to accept the new service book, even though they had described it as but 'like a Christmas game'.

St Keverne parish has an extensive and rugged coastline with the small settlements of Porthallow and Porthoustock with its granite quarries and further south the fishing village of Coverack. The gentle scenery of the Helford estuary disappears as we round Nare Point and face the sea, and as we go south along the coast so the scenery becomes grander. Coverack now has a good deal of modern building, but the older part retains its character as a typical Cornish fishing village.

Inland St Keverne presents even more contrasting landscape. To the north are the fields and woods of the Meneage area, but to the south of the road from Helston to Coverack the land becomes flat and bare. This is part of Goonhilly Downs, a plateau occupying the centre of the Lizard peninsula, and a region of an entirely individual character. Its natural centre, on slightly higher ground, is at Dry Tree, close to what is now the dominant feature of the landscape. The name Goonhilly suddenly became well known in 1962 when the Post Office set up a radio satellite tracking station here, its three huge bowls visible over a large area of south and west Cornwall. But this was clearly a focal point in earlier days, since several parish boundaries meet here. The blaze of gorse covering the Downs in spring gives way in late summer to the Cornish heath, *erica vagans,* and the botanist can find many unusual flowers and heathers in the district.

A walker following the coastal footpath south from Coverack has a sequence of cliff scenery and a headland castle at Carrick Luz, then a stretch of beach at Kennack Sands. A stream from Goonhilly Downs enters the sea at the picturesque Poltesco Valley, and a mile or so further on is the attractive little fishing harbour of Cadgwith. Several churches in this area, Grade, Ruan Minor, Landewednack, and other buildings as well make considerable use of serpentine, the most distinctive rock of the peninsula. This is usually green, occasionally grey or red, with veins which supposedly give it the appearance of a serpent's skin. While it has been useful as a building material—Truro Cathedral contains some—its principal function now is to supply craftsmen, particularly at the Lizard Town, with the material for a thriving souvenir industry. The stone polishes well, and ashtrays and lighthouses are attractive and popular items in the gift shops.

The church of Grade near Cadgwith contains memorials of the Erisey family whose manor house lies away from the road north of the now ruined church of Ruan Major. The family was an ancient one; one of its members was James Erisey, commander of the *White Lion* on Drake's West Indies Expedition of 1585.

Landewednack is the church of the Lizard, the most southerly point in the country. A lighthouse guards this tip of England, as well it needs to with the tumble of jagged rocks against which the sea continually foams. Lizard Point marks the eastern extremity of Mount's Bay, and as we continue along the coast more of the bay comes into view. Several stretches of this fine coast are in the care of the National Trust, including Kynance Cove, a mile or so from the Lizard. The scenery here is renowned for its grandeur, with Steeple Rock and Asparagus Island rising from the water, fascinating caves, and much to interest the geologist and the collector of pebbles.

The coast path continues its spectacular way northward, with more of the coastline coming into view as Predannack Head is rounded. Inland from here on the plateau an airfield was laid out, and to the north of it is the sizeable village of Mullion, a residential and tourist centre. The church is remarkable for its woodwork. There is original timber in the wagon roofs, and some original work in the largely modern screen. But the finest possession is the set of bench-ends, possibly the best series in the whole county. The designs include initials, the symbols of the Passion, such as the crown of thorns, the spear, the scourge, nails and dice, and human figures such as a monk and a jester.

At nearby Poldhu Cove there is a monument to Marconi, who brought the name of Poldhu to public notice at the beginning of the century by transmitting the first message to America from the radio station here. Beyond the golf course is Church Cove, Gunwalloe, where the cliffs give way to gently sloping towans, and a stream idles down to the sea. Few churches in Cornwall have so unusual a setting, practically on the beach but sheltered from the sea by a small headland. Detached from the building and growing out of the hillside is a bell tower with a pyramidal roof, built to house the usual medieval complement of three bells.

It was not until the eighteenth century that much attempt was made to increase the number of bells in Cornish towers. At that time, however, a large number of bells were cast, very often on the site rather than at a foundry, and a corresponding interest in ringing grew. Several towers preserve boards with ringers' rules, penalising incompetent ringing or irreverent behaviour. Campanology thrives in Cornwall today, the art of change ringing being practised more in the western part of the county. Several churches are centres for ringers, and Truro Cathedral has a noble ring of ten.

Inland from Gunwalloe is the church linked with it, Cury, set in a small hamlet in a commanding position. Architecturally its interest lies in a fine Norman south doorway surmounted by a tympanum, and a squint connecting the chancel with the south transept. Ecclesiastically it acquired some notoriety early in this century during the incumbency of the eccentric Fr Sandys Wason, who was sadly persecuted for ritualistic practices and the use of the Latin Mass, and eventually deprived.

While we might hear the sound of bells in the distance, a more regular sound in this area comes from the aerial activity at H.M.S. *Seahawk*, the Royal Naval Air Station at Culdrose on the outskirts of Helston. This important base is a training establishment for helicopter pilots, and the sight and sound of their machines is now almost a feature of the landscape. Certainly the presence of a large air base so close to Helston has had a considerable effect on the town and its economy.

In the early thirteenth century the town of Helston became a borough, occupying a strategic position on the Cober ('stream') commanding the entrance to the southern peninsula. Originally Henliston (*hen-lis*, the old court), its trade received a setback when the formation of the Loe Bar at the mouth of the Cober cut it off from the sea. It was at this juncture that the town acquired the little port of Gweek on the nearby Helford River as an alternative. This was its main link with the world at large in medieval times. Centuries later a branch railway line was opened in 1887, connecting the town with the main line west of Camborne at Gwinear Road, though this line closed in 1962.

A hilly town, Helston preserves an attractive character with a number of Georgian and Regency buildings. The focal point is the granite Market House of 1839, built in the classical style with columns on the upper storey. From here the wide Coinagehall Street (recalling its days as a stannary town) curves down the hill towards the river; the view downhill is completed by a Gothic entrance arch to a public park, set up in 1834. Notable among the buildings in this street is the old town house of the Godolphin family, now the Angel Hotel.

From the Market House, Church Street runs at right angles to Coinagehall Street, downhill and up the other side of a valley to the church of St Michael. This is not a typical Cornish church; a previous building suffered considerable storm damage early in the eighteenth century, and so a few years later a completely new church was built in the classicial style, to the design of Thomas Edwards, through the generosity of the Earl of Godolphin. The interior arrangement has recently been reorganized.

It was the dedication to St Michael which gave the town its

principal annual event. May 8th is a festival of the archangel, and that day sees an influx of visitors to witness the Furry Dance for which the town is famed. Helston's spring ritual is a more elegant affair than Padstow's, with the formally-dressed dancers winding their way through the streets and houses to the sound of the ancient tune played by the hard-working band. By way of contrast, a plaque in the town commemorates the birthplace of Bob Fitzsimmons, the last British boxer to hold the title of World Heavyweight Champion.

Having passed Helston, the River Cober flows through the Loe valley and then enters the Loe Pool, the largest natural freshwater lake in Cornwall, now in the care of the National Trust. Penned in behind the shingle bank of the Loe Bar, the water spreads back in two arms, Carminow Creek and the Loe Pool itself, fringed with the woods of the Penrose estate. A culvert now allows the water to escape to the sea, but before its construction heavy rain could result in flooding in the lower parts of Helston. It was also claimed that Loe Pool was the genuine site, 'the shining levels of the lake', where Arthur's sword Excalibur was returned to its home. Tennyson found inspiration while visiting Cornwall, and perhaps the memory of the Loe Bar remained with him.

'*a dark strait of barren land:*
On one side lay the Ocean, and on one
Lay a great water, and the moon was full'.

On a peaceful night of still moonlight it is not difficult to imagine how Sir Bedivere 'paced beside the mere, counting the dewy pebbles' and how 'the great brand made lightnings in the splendour of the moon'.

The River Cober rises ten miles away on the shoulder of Carnmenellis, and flows through Porkellis Moor and by the village of Wendron. This is now isolated and lonely country, though formerly a tin-mining district. Wendron was once the mother church of Helston, and has a granite tower and a battlemented porch. Canon G. H. Doble, rector for 20 years from 1925, established a reputation not only in this country but in Europe as an authority on Celtic saints, and wrote the lives of many, based on his discoveries of early medieval biographies.

The mines of this area lay in a belt to the south of Wendron and Porkellis, and west of Helston was another mining district. This area lay roughly in a triangle bounded by Leedstown, Porthleven and Marazion, and produced both tin and copper. The

landscape is dominated by the granite mass of Tregonning and
Godolphin Hills, and nearby was the extremely productive tin
mine of Great Wheal Vor. The greatest yields of copper came
from Crenver and Wheal Abraham, near Leedstown, so named
after the Duke of Leeds, into whose possession the Godolphin
estates passed in 1785.

Among the mining parishes are the neighbours of Breage and
Germoe. The fifteenth-century granite church at Breage is notable
for its wall-paintings, and preserves one of the few Roman mile-
stones found in Cornwall, dating from the mid-3rd century. In
Germoe churchyard is a curious building known as St Germoe's
Chair, consisting of three seats under a canopy supported by granite columns, and south of the village near Praa Sands is the
medieval peel tower of Pengersick Castle.

North of Germoe rises Godolphin Hill, and beyond it, among
woods stretching down to the River Hayle, is Godolphin Hall.
This two-storey building, home of the Godolphin family, dates
mainly from the seventeenth century, with some older parts. The
approach is from the north, and here is a granite battlemented front
with a colonnade behind Tuscan columns. The grey old building in
its quiet surroundings below the hill expresses solidity, as firm as the
nearby land whose mineral wealth was the basis of the family's
prosperity, as John Leland found on his visit here in 1538.

A notable member of the family was the Cavalier poet, Sidney
Godolphin, whose character was described by Clarendon: 'there
was never so great a mind and spirit contained in so little room'.
Retiring and quiet by disposition, he was nevertheless among the
first to take up arms for the King when the Civil War broke out,
and 'bore the uneasiness and fatigue of winter marches with an
exemplary courage and alacrity'. He was not destined to survive
the wretched war: a stray shot struck him during a skirmish at
Chagford in Devon, and a young life of much charm and ability
was extinguished.

Two years later there was born another Sidney Godolphin who
rose to positions of eminence in affairs of state, and was created
first Earl of Godolphin. He was a page at Court—Charles II
favoured the family who had given him refuge in the Isles of Scilly
during the war—and became member of Parliament for Helston.
Throughout the political upheaval towards the end of the century
he continued to rise in power as a diplomat and a commissioner of
the Treasury. He came into his own in the reign of Queen Anne,

being appointed Lord Treasurer in 1702. A supporter of Marlborough, he financed the wars in which the Duke achieved his successes, from Blenheim to Malplaquet. Although losing favour and being dismissed in 1710, two years before his death, he served his country well for many years.

Porthleven harbour was developed in the early nineteenth century, but it was never a successful port for nearby Helston since it faces directly south-west, and access was frequently difficult. This part of Mount's Bay has some stretches of beach, such as Praa Sands and Perran Sands near Perranuthnoe, but also has rocky headlands and cliffs which threaten any vessel sheltering in the bay and caught by the south-west winds on the lee shore. The Cornish coastline as a whole, with its numerous bays and headlands, has a long history of shipwrecks, and this coast of Mount's Bay in particular has proved very treacherous. In former times not only the area but also the inhabitants acquired notoriety. Wrecking was certainly not limited to Cornwall, any more than shipwrecks, but the practice became widespread here for various reasons, such as the remoteness of the area and the general poverty of the population.

However, we must be clear what is meant by 'wrecking'. The notion of men of murderous intent showing lights on shore to deceive vessels at night is probably more in the realms of fiction than in real life. On the other hand when Sir John Killigrew in the early seventeenth century proposed to build a lighthouse at the Lizard (not out of altruism—he intended to charge dues from ships passing the light), there was a tremendous outcry from the neighbouring population. They feared that no more shipwrecks would occur on their shore, and these had been a regular feature of their economy.

Whenever news spread that a wreck was imminent, the crowds would gather like vultures, waiting for the luckless vessels to come to shore. For tinners in particular this became part of their way of life, and they regarded wrecks as providential Acts of God to alleviate their normal wretched conditions. Once aground, a vessel would soon be plundered of its cargo, men, women and children often taking part, and frequently the ship itself would be dismantled. All this would usually be done in haste before the arrival of Customs officials or the military, frequently in the dark and at no small risk to the wreckers themselves. In rough weather it is not difficult to recreate in the imagination scenes which must have been all too common in the seventeenth and eighteenth centuries. On the other hand it is heartening to read accounts of efforts made to help ships in distress.

On 29 December 1807, the frigate *Anson* was driven ashore on Loe Bar, and heeled over, pounded by huge waves. Some of those on board escaped to land, but many more were swept away by the tremendous seas, before the eyes of helpless spectators on the shore. Among these was a Helston man, Henry Trengrouse, who left the scene determined to try to devise a means of preventing such tragedies as the one he had witnessed. A firework display suggested an idea to him. A rocket might carry a light line between a ship and the shore, to which a rope could be secured and a means of escape thereby achieved. Trengrouse worked on his apparatus and produced a convenient rocket device for the purpose. Then followed many years of frustration before his device was officially accepted, involving considerable expense on the part of Trengrouse. However, to his satisfaction though not his financial benefit, the apparatus was adopted, and innumerable lives saved as a result.

The coast of Mount's Bay was also one of the areas where smuggling took place on quite a large scale. It became a regular activity in the late seventeenth century, when the nation embarked on wars, chiefly for trading reasons, and import duties became an important source of income. To combat such illegal activity, the Board of Customs was set up and the Preventive Service came into operation, though throughout the eighteenth century it was frequently proved that officers, and the crews of revenue vessels, were not above accepting bribes. After the Napoleonic Wars finally ended and the government could devote more time and energy to countering the smugglers, so the tactics changed: instead of landing their cargoes directly, goods would be sunk in marked locations, to be moved when opportunity arose. Eventually, as 'free trading' became unprofitable and not worth the risks, authority gained the upper hand.

Cornwall was, of course, well suited for smuggling, with its miles of coastline and general inaccessibility. Cornish fishermen were ideally equipped for running cargoes, since they were skilled at handling suitable craft and had an intimate knowledge of their own part of the coast, which was essential, particularly in some of the smaller coves and inlets. It was important that there should be a ready market for disposal of the goods, which was one reason

why the north coast east of Padstow was not much frequented by
smugglers; in addition, this coast has few suitable landing places.
West of Padstow the north coast afforded several suitable landing
places, such as St Ives, with its constant activity, and the Hayle
estuary, and smaller, inhospitable sites such as Hell's Mouth. Old
mine workings were useful for storing goods, and mining towns
such as Camborne were not far inland.

But the south coast offered great opportunities, and from
Mount's Bay to Cawsand Bay cargoes found their way regularly
ashore. Near Falmouth there was always a great deal of sailing
activity which made detection more difficult, so the harbours of
the Lizard peninsula, from Gunwalloe to Coverack, and the quiet
Helford River, were frequent scenes of illegal landings. The various creeks of the Fal estuary were used, and Falmouth itself was
very much a centre since the Packet Service combined its official
duties with smuggling activities almost as a matter of course. The
south-east coast was particularly engaged in the trade, especially
Polperro and Cawsand Bay, where luggers were actually built for
the purpose. Many cargoes were taken directly across the Channel
and landed here, dangerously under the nose of the Customs
authorities at Devonport, but at the same time convenient for the
market at Plymouth.

Many colourful characters left legends behind them, perhaps
none more remarkable than the Carters of Prussia Cove. John
Carter acquired the title 'King of Prussia' during boyhood games,
and it stayed with him as he became the natural and respected
leader of the smuggling activities of the little cove. His brother
Harry spent his time at sea, running the cargoes across from
France, while John saw to their storage and disposal. A legendary
exploit, which is also a comment on his character, occurred when
during his absence excise officers seized a newly-run cargo and
impounded it at Penzance. John Carter thereupon led a party
which broke into the store and retrieved his goods—and scrupul-
ously left intact anything which was not part of the cargo.

Inland from Perranuthnoe is the parish of St Hilary, lying to
the west of the River Hayle. The churchtown of small granite
houses lies at the end of a lane among trees, with the spire of the
church peeping out between them. Only the tower with its broach
spire survives from the medieval building destroyed by fire in the
middle of the nineteenth century; the body of the church was
rebuilt by William White, and lies low with an atmosphere of

mystery. In the early years of this century it was enriched by several paintings by local artists, encouraged by the vicar of the time, Bernard Walke.

This remarkable and much loved man was vicar from 1912 to 1932, and related his experiences in *Twenty Years at St Hilary*. Like his friend Sandys Wason at Cury, he suffered from persecutors who felt it their Christian duty to discourage his ritualistic practices by hiring men to wreck the church. But what spread the fame of the parish on a national scale was the series of Nativity plays which he wrote and directed and which were relayed to the country in the early days of broadcasting. These were not professional performances, but the sincere efforts of ordinary parishioners, adults and children, their Cornish voices conveying the message of Christmas into the homes of the land in a way that was direct, fresh and profoundly moving.

From St Hilary the road to the west brings us down to the narrow streets of the former borough of Marazion, whose significance in earlier centuries lay in its position on the trade route from the River Hayle to Mount's Bay, and later as a gathering point for pilgrims. Now it is the tourist who follows in the steps of the medieval pilgrim, turning his gaze to the bay and one of the wonders of Cornwall, St Michael's Mount. This is an island at high tide but connected by a causeway with the mainland at low water. Legend furnished it with a giant, Cormoran, and its romantic situation is the type of setting to inspire legends. Its dedication to St Michael was the result of an appearance of the archangel to some fishermen here in the 6th century.

Pilgrims were attracted to the Mount, and in 1044 a Benedictine Priory was established here by Edward the Confessor, though building probably did not take place until some years later. After 1425, when the Priory was suppressed as alien, the emphasis gradually altered from religious to military, with the Mount playing a part in the Wars of the Roses and in the rebellion of Perkin Warbeck. With the Suppression of the Monasteries it passed into royal hands, a valuable strategic possession with its useful and busy harbour and its commanding situation. During the Civil War the Mount was defended for the Royalists by the Basset family who owned it, but during the Commonwealth period it came into the hands of the St Aubyns of Clowance. In 1954 it was presented by Lord St Levan to the National Trust, and now receives thousands of visitors each year.

The Mount is about a mile in circumference, with a harbour and piers on the landward side, together with groups of houses. The picturesque castle dominates the height of the rock, rising above the trees and the sub-tropical gardens planted in the nineteenth century. A fair amount of conversion and rebuilding has been necessary over the years to turn monastic buildings into a residence. The refectory became what is now known as the Chevy Chase Room on account of its seventeenth-century frieze with hunting scenes, and in the eighteenth century the Lady Chapel at the east end of the church was turned into two elegant drawing-rooms. A century later the family architect J. P. St Aubyn made some spectacular additions on the south-east, which gave more accommodation without destroying the magnificent outline of the composition as a whole.

St Michael's Mount is the focal point of Mount's Bay, spectacular and romantic in all weathers. Perhaps it is at its grandest when seen from the nearby shore, backed by the full sweep of the sea, its towers and battlements crowning the skyline. Nature and architecture together provide a magnificent composition, and leave a lasting impression on all who see it, all who remember

'Where the great Vision of the guarded Mount
Looks toward Namancos and Bayona's hold'.

NINE

The Far West

The coastal strip extending for about two miles along the northern shore of Mount's Bay is an area of intensive cultivation of flowers and vegetables. A mild climate and a sheltered aspect combine to make these acres highly productive, notably in the early months of the year. The first crop is the winter cauliflower, broccoli, the peak of the season being from the middle of February to early March; this is followed by the planting of early potatoes ready for the market in late May and early June. The region also produces quantities of flowers, particularly daffodils, narcissi, anemones and violets, for the most part grown in the open air. It is no surprise to find that one of the most remarkable of Cornish gardens was that of Ludgvan Rectory, where Canon Boscawen tended rare plants from China and New Zealand.

Ludgvan lies above the east end of the market garden belt, looking down on the southern end of the ancient trade route across the peninsula. This old route is still the course of both road and railway, since to the north-west the land rises steadily to the heights of inland Penwith. The sea is never far away in this western peninsula; only one parish, Sancreed, does not touch the coast, and from much of the high ground the sea is visible, sometimes both to north and south.

The village of Ludgvan with its square of stone cottages and granite church tower is very attractive, and from its hillside commands a wonderful view of St Michael's Mount. It was here that the eighteenth-century antiquary William Borlase was rector for 50 years, a conscientious parson with many interests, especially the natural history of the county, and above all the prehistoric remains of the Penwith area. Though sharing in the delusions about the Druids common in the eighteenth century, he was an extremely fine topographical archaeologist. With the subsequent disappearance or deterioration of some of the monuments, his acute observation and his high standard of draughtsmanship were of permanent value: his *Cornish Antiquities* was published in 1753, and his *Natural History* four years later.

Two miles west of Ludgvan is the village of Gulval, similarly situated where the land starts to rise from the fertile plain. Again the village is attractive, and the churchyard is notable for its luxuriant vegetation. Half a mile to the south is the airport where helicopters maintain a regular service to the Isles of Scilly, offering a bird's eye view of west Cornwall in the process. The other regular link with the islands is the steamer service; the journey is comparatively short, but the meeting of currents off Land's End often produces a notorious turbulence which challenges the constitution of the most hardened traveller.

The mainland port for the Scillies is Penzance, which is also the western terminus of the railway and indeed the most westerly town of any size in Cornwall, occupying a sheltered position on the north-west side of Mount's Bay. The arrival of the railway was the making of modern Penzance as the tourist centre for the western peninsula, just as it gave a tremendous boost to the market gardening of the area. The town is comparatively recent in its development and its buildings. Its early life was as a fishing village, but nothing survives from medieval times since a Spanish landing party burnt it to the ground in 1595. Penzance acquired some importance in the seventeenth century when it became the coinage town for the western mining area, but it is chiefly a Regency town with the various developments of our own time. Above the harbour with its varied activities rises the granite tower of St Mary's church, built in 1834 to replace the former chapel which stood on the site—a sign of the developing importance of the town. Not until 1871, however, was it a parish church: the mother church is inland at Madron.

From the railway station the harbour road rounds the headland to the Promenade, while the main street, Market Jew Street (*Yow*, Thursday), climbs its curving way to the Market House with its pillared portico and dome. A walk around the town will discover many attractive terraces and houses of the Georgian and Regency period, including the Egyptian House designed by Foulston in

Chapel Street. Westward along the sea front spread the hotels and boarding houses, with their view over the Bay beyond the Promenade, an unusual feature for a Cornish town. But then Penzance itself with its terraces and sub-tropical shrubs and palms fits somewhat incongruously with its stern hinterland of bare granite uplands.

In front of the Market House stands the statue of Sir Humphry Davy, a Cornishman of genius. A lively personality with a questing mind, he did more than live 'in the odium of having discovered sodium', though he certainly did make this discovery and that of potassium in 1807. He is not now generally thought of as a poet, though his gifts impressed Scott, Wordsworth, Coleridge and Southey; the achievement by which he is best remembered is the invention of the Miners' Safety Lamp, an enormous blessing to the coal-mining world. Four years later, in 1820, he became President of the Royal Society, his successor being his fellow-Cornishman Davies Gilbert of St Erth.

Madron, on the road climbing the hill behind the town, commands a view over Mount's Bay to the distant Goonhilly Downs; its granite church contains monuments to Penzance families and woodwork of several periods. North-west of the village is the interesting old Madron Well with its ruined chapel, while to the south-east is Trengwainton House, its grounds cared for by the National Trust and containing many rare sub-tropical plants in its walled garden.

The Spanish raids of July 1595 destroyed not only the fishing village of Penzance but its neighbours on the western side of Mount's Bay, Newlyn and Mousehole, and the churchtown of Paul inland on the hillside. Paul church was extensively damaged by fire during the raid; it is dedicated, not to the Apostle of the Gentiles, but to the Breton St Pol de Leon. Close by are eighteenth-century almshouses, and near the churchyard gate is a monument to Dolly Pentreath who died at a ripe age in 1778. She was reputed to be the last person to speak the Cornish language as her mother tongue, though this claim is disputed.

A valley runs down from Paul to Mousehole, the picturesque fishing harbour once known as Port Enys. Only Keigwin manor house survived the Spanish raid, and remains today with its pillared porchway and granite windows. The cave known as the Mousehole is just south of the town, near Point Spaniard. The little harbour is as secluded as its name suggests; it nestles under the hillside in the lee of the westerly winds, and is sheltered from the open sea by piers extending from either side like protecting arms.

The coast road from Mousehole runs past the Penlee quarries to the port of Newlyn, now almost part of Penzance but with a long history as a fishing settlement on its own. From the eighteenth century it grew in importance as one of the leading centres for landing mackerel, pilchards and herrings. In the nineteenth century the harbour was greatly increased in size by the construction of new piers, the southern one now holding an Ordnance Survey Tidal Observatory. At the same period the fishing industry received the same boost as other concerns when the railway connection was opened, providing regular fast transport for the catches; Penzance became the rail centre for Newlyn as well as the other major fishing port in west Cornwall, St Ives.

Fishing has been part of the Cornish scene for centuries, though for various reasons its great days are past, and Cornish fishermen now face even keener competition. For many years, when the principal Cornish toast was 'Fish, tin and copper', St Ives dominated the north coast fishing grounds, while the south coast had fishing fleets in every cove and inlet from Plymouth Sound to the far west. Before the turn of this century pilchards were the mainstay of the Cornish industry, and seining the traditional method of their capture.

The pilchard season was roughly from August to October, or as the saying went,

> *'When the corn is in the shock,*
> *Then the fish is on the rock.'*

Methods changed little over the centuries. When the time drew near for the shoals of fish to approach the coast, a 'huer' or watchman took up his station at a vantage point above the sea—the huer's house at Newquay is a well-known reminder of this important individual. When he saw the signs of a shoal's arrival, he alerted the boats' crews with his shout of 'Hevva, hevva' (the Cornish word for a shoal) and directed them into position by signals. Finally he gave the sign for shooting the seine net, and the work of landing the fish began.

Since it was essential to work quickly, the whole community took part, landing the glistening catch and salting it, ready to be preserved for winter consumption or for transport to the seaports and the journey to the Mediterranean. Little was exported to England, the bulk went to Italy and Spain: 'Long life to the Pope' was the Cornish fishermen's toast, 'and death to the thousands'. It is incredible to think that on occasions millions of fish were landed at St Ives within an hour: small wonder that the vicar told the diarist Francis Kilvert that the smell of fish was sometimes so powerful as to stop the church clock. But in the early years of this century the pilchards deserted the inshore Cornish waters: the huer's voice was silenced, and the seining vessels were eventually broken up.

It is not only fishing which links Newlyn and St Ives. At the end of the nineteenth century, as the growth of tourism brought more visitors, painters recognized the particularly appealing qualities which have made the far west a home for artists—scenery both grand and picturesque, an unusual clarity of light and an indefinable power and magic in what seemed a haunted land. Artists soon settled at St Ives, and at Newlyn a school developed, influenced by the French Impressionists, living in cottages in streets such as that renamed the 'Rue des Beaux Arts'. From here came the memorable scenes of fishing life produced by Stanhope Forbes, the founder of the school, and paintings such as Frank Bramley's 'A Hopeless Dawn'. Artists settled and worked in many parts of Cornwall, and the local people came to accept them as part of the Cornish scene. St Ives is now the acknowledged art centre of Cornwall, with artists working in a variety of styles, traditional and experimental.

As the Hayle estuary became silted up, St Ives took advantage of its situation at the western end of the bay to develop as the principal harbour on this coast. It was also a mining centre, the miners living in the Stennack on the slopes above the Downalong where the fishing community had their homes, and it was among these people that John Wesley began his first preaching mission in Cornwall in 1743. As the industries declined, so the Great Western Railway providentially brought the branch railway line from St Erth; and with the railway came the town's new role as one of Cornwall's principal tourist centres. The railway line runs past the old village of Lelant, and then follows the coast with splendid views over the bay. Carbis Bay has developed largely with the growth of the holiday industry; it has a fine modern church, designed on traditional Cornish lines, and notable as the only church in the county (except for Truro Cathedral) with a ring of ten bells. The railway continues to wind along the edge of the coast to the terminus above the sands of Porthminster Beach.

The old fishing quarter of St Ives occupies the neck of land leading to the promontory known as the Island, an ideal vantage point for surveying the coast and for watching sea-birds. To the west is the spread of Porthmeor Beach, and on the sheltered eastern side is the harbour, flanked by Smeaton's pier of 1767. Care has been taken to preserve the character of the buildings in this quarter of the town; it is a place to explore on foot, with plenty of time to spare, as a succession of alleys and courtyards attract attention. It was not until 1826 that St Ives gained her ecclesiastical independence from Lelant, though she had possessed a chapel of ease since the early fifteenth century. However, this was not the usual small building so often serving the harbour communities of the county but the large church of St Ia whose grand four-stage tower is so essential a feature of the harbour skyline. Its screen did not survive Puritan zeal in the seventeenth century, but there is old woodwork in the roofs, pulpit and bench-ends; the figure of the Virgin and Child by Barbara Hepworth in the Lady Chapel makes a striking contrast.

St Ives and Penzance guard the northern and southern approaches to Penwith and are the western-most major centres of population. It is possible to take the coast road from St Ives and work round the peninsula to Penzance, and even better to follow the more strenuous course of walking the coastal footpath. Splendid though this granite coast is, however, one would not be justified in claiming a knowledge of the area without exploring the country inland. Much of this is the stern landscape one would expect of an area of granite uplands, but this district has the greatest concentration of ancient monuments in the country. Indeed there are so many important sites in the area that it is worth considering them collectively before looking at other aspects of the peninsula.

The Neolithic period has left several cromlechs which mark the burial places of chieftains. Little else survives from this time but these massive structures remain as witness to the awe in which their builders held the mystery of death. Like Trethevy Quoit in east Cornwall, they were originally covered with earthen mounds which have gradually disappeared, leaving the bare granite bones of the burial chamber exposed. Near Zennor are the ruined remains of Sperris Quoit, and a quarter of a mile away the larger structure of Zennor Quoit. Like its neighbour on Mulfra Hill, this was once covered by a round barrow and has its capstone resting on the ground at one end.

Two miles south-west of Mulfra Quoit is one of the most spectacular cromlechs, Lanyon Quoit, which is in the care of the National Trust. It is not actually as its original builders left it, since in 1815 its capstone fell and was later re-erected. The tripod form of this cromlech contrasts with the mushroom shape of Chun Quoit, on a lonely hillside south of Morvah. In the open country north of Lanyon Quoit is the curious Men-an-Tol, or holed stone. Set between two upright pillars is a circular stone, once perhaps the entrance to a burial chamber. Whatever its original function, later superstition endowed it with miraculous healing properties for those who passed through the hole. The strange relic keeps its secret, with Lanyon Quoit standing on the southern horizon, and to the east the melancholy engine-house of the desolate Ding Dong mine.

Within half a mile or so of the Men-an-Tol is the stone circle known as the Nine Maidens. The name is a comparatively recent invention, a moralising corruption of the Cornish *maen*, a stone; 'nine' is also a conventional description since there are more than that number of stones here and at the other circles similarly named. Two of the finest circles are to be seen in the neighbourhood of St Buryan. At Boscawen-Un there is a central stone inclining at a steep angle and 19 uprights all in place, the same number as at the Merry Maidens circle near the hamlet of Boleigh. The circles are probably relics of the second millenium B.C., though one can only guess at their purpose; it is certainly daunting to consider how many centuries have turned while these stones remained in their position.

In 1928 the circle at Boscawen-Un was chosen as the setting for the first Gorsedd of Cornish bards, revived largely under the leadership of the venerable Cornish scholar Henry Jenner. The picturesque gathering is held annually at different sites in the county, and has contributed materially to the renewed interest in Cornish culture and history, never stronger than today. One notable aspect is the increasing study of the Cornish language; this was once widely spoken in the county but by Carew's time the English tongue had driven it 'into the uttermost skirts of the shire'. Its renaissance is now a reality: church services entirely in Cornish might be considered an off-beat Celtic fringe activity, but to attend such a service within a church whose builders spoke the tongue is a deeply moving experience.

In addition to the standing stones such as the Pipers are such isolated menhirs as the Men Scryfa near the Men-an-Tol, but inscribed stones of this type are much later, from the years following the Roman period. By this time the hill-top fortifications of the Iron Age had been in existence for several centuries. We have already seen Trencrom Hill at the eastern end of the Penwith uplands; and on the hill-top inland from Ludgvan and Gulval is Castle-an-Dinas West. Near Sancreed is Caer Brane, while three miles to the north is the most elaborate of all, Chun Castle. Two formidable granite-faced ramparts protected the inner enclosure, the entrances being staggered to make attack the more difficult. The citadel must have been well-nigh impregnable, and seems to have been occupied for several centuries, before and after the Roman occupation of Britain, by which time Chun Quoit on the hillside to the west had already been in position for over 1,000 years. Allied to the hill-top sites are the promontory forts, which we have noticed in many parts of the county. Among the most notable in Penwith are the long headland of Gurnard's Head near Zennor, Maen Castle near Land's End and Treryn Dinas on the south coast, the last two both being on stretches of the coast held by the National Trust.

With the passing of the centuries it is not easy to associate these ancient remains with their human builders or occupants; cromlechs, circles and hill forts now seem almost part of the natural landscape. Perhaps we can approach a little nearer to the people of 2,000 years ago when we visit the sites of the villages containing groups of courtyard houses. Often the original inhabitants of these villages lived in huts built of timber and turf, but later generations built more elaborate and permanent stone houses. Several of these sites have been found in the area, the most extensive remains being at Chysauster on the western slopes of Castle-an-Dinas and at Carn Euny near Sancreed. Here at Carn Euny is a stone-lined fogou, 66 feet long, with a side chamber branching off at its eastern end.

Chysauster shows most clearly the pattern of courtyard houses, consisting of a street with four houses on each side, and a fogou nearby. The village itself was not fortified; the defensive position, if needed, was on the summit of the hill. Each house is approached from the east, the side sheltered from the prevailing wind. A passage opens into a central court, about 30 feet across, around which are several chambers, with living and working accommodation and perhaps stabling for animals. The principal support of the roof seems to have been a post in the main living room; roofing materials probably varied, and drainage channels can be traced. Here, while most of Britain was under Roman domination and influence, Celtic farmers lived a comparatively settled life, with tin-streaming probably varying the agricultural activities. The present and the past seem very much in touch here; despite the passing of so many centuries, one has the impression that only recently was the village a thriving and busy community.

On the slopes inland from St Ives is the mining settlement of Halsetown, whose rows of early nineteenth-century cottages were built by James Halse, a St Ives mine-owner. To the west are the open uplands of the parish of Towednack; granite boulders line the wandering lanes, and the little church crouches by its two-stage tower. Rosewall Hill and Trendrine Hill guard the road north towards the sea, and beyond them the coast road follows its winding course to the grey granite village of Zennor. This mining settlement was regularly visited by the early Methodists—both the Wesleys preached here—and in the church is a bench-end with a mermaid; the legend tells how she was attracted by the singing of the squire's son and lured him after her to a watery death.

From Zennor Head we can see the unmistakable promontory of Gurnard's Head with its headland fortification, and inland rise the heights of the Penwith massif, Watch Croft, Carn Galver and Hannibal's Carn. Beyond Gurnard's Head are some of the finest rock-climbing cliffs in the country, and the path through the granite boulders and the bracken of the National Trust's Rosemergy stretch of coastline brings us to Morvah, 'the place by the sea'. Westward of the village a road runs out past the Borlase family home with its fogou to the headland of Pendeen Watch; since the beginning of this century a lighthouse has guarded the north-west shoulder of the peninsula.

We are now in the western mining area, with the gaunt ruins of engine-houses perched dramatically on the edge of the cliffs, among them the famous Levant and Botallack mines. Here some of the levels extended beneath the sea, and miners working there could sometimes hear the distant roar of the Atlantic above their heads. Levant mine is now worked in conjunction with Geevor at St Just, one of the mines still operative in west Cornwall. Along the road spread the rows of miners' cottages at Pendeen, and above them rises the tower of the church, approached through a battlemented gateway. The building dates from 1851, the work of miners themselves under the direction of their evangelical vicar, Robert Aitken, a powerful personality who designed the church himself.

The capital of this mining world is St Just, a bleak, grey little town of chapels and stone buildings, with streets radiating from the focal point of Bank Square. To one side is the fifteenth-century granite church, and here also is the plan-an-gwary or amphitheatre where medieval plays were performed; later it was used by Methodist preachers, and also for bouts of Cornish wrestling, both activities attracting large numbers of miners. From St Just the road runs down to Cape Cornwall, a conical headland crowned with a mine chimney. This is the southern end of the stretch of metamorphosed greenstone extending to Pendeen Watch and containing the tin and copper lodes: the junction of the slate and the granite is very noticeable here at Priest's Cove.

A mile out to sea the waves break around the dangerous Brisons, and a rugged coast stretches south to the broad sweep of Whitesand Bay and the little harbour of Sennen Cove. The bay is no longer the remote place it was when Stephen landed here in 1135 nor even when Perkin Warbeck stepped ashore in 1497, but the little cove is most attractive and the cliffs continue their grand way to Land's End.

The northern coast of the peninsula is grimly spectacular; the southern shore is equally fine and offers several coves in contrast to the rocky headlands. A couple of miles south-west of Mousehole the granite cliffs begin at Carn-du, at the eastern end of the inlet of Lamorna Cove. A narrow lane runs down the luxuriant valley to the sea, accompanied by a stream whose headwaters are in the parish of Sancreed near the Drift Reservoir. Tin mines were formerly worked in this parish, which contains a wealth of ancient monuments, including two important Celtic crosses with carved decoration and inscriptions.

Most of the southern part of this peninsula is dominated by the grand tower of St Buryan church, set in a commanding position and visible for miles around, even from the Isles of Scilly over 30 miles away. The church itself is the finest in the area, built of granite, with tall arcades, old stalls with misericords and a splendid screen running across the whole width of the building. The

stalls are a survival from St Buryan's collegiate days; tradition
links its founding with King Athelstan. Certainly in the Middle
Ages this was a Royal Peculiar, in the care of a Dean appointed
by the Duchy of Cornwall; only in 1864 did this system come to an
end, though the college of priests had been dissolved in 1545 when
such establishments were seized by the Crown.

To the west of Lamorna Cove is the lighthouse at Tater-du and
the next break in the cliffs is where a stream comes down to the
sea at Penberth. This is an active little fishing settlement, despite
the heavy seas which can roll in against the rocks and send the
spray flying over the securely-moored boats and the granite cottages. The National Trust owns the coast on either side of the
cove, including the stretch to the west which contains the headland of Treryn Dinas, where Tennyson and his friends walked and
where Palgrave resolved to start compiling *The Golden Treasury*.
The headland is best reached from the hamlet of Treen; a path
leads over the fields to the cliffs and the defensive works of the
promontory castle with its famous Logan Rock, or rocking stone.
The craggy headland is seen at its best from the sheltered sandy
beach of Porthcurno at the western end of the bay.

The village developed with the establishment of the Cable and
Wireless school here at the terminus of the Atlantic cable, though
this is further up the valley away from the sea, where the road
swings round to the church of St Levan. The parish covers the
south-western corner of the peninsula and the church lies tucked
into its hillside above the stream which runs past St Levan's Well
on its way down to Porth Chapel beach.

Between Porthcurno and the headland of Pedn-mên-an-mere is
the Minack Theatre, a Cornish Epidaurus on the cliffside. This
dates from the 1930's when Miss Rowena Cade of Minack House
saw the possibilities of the site and enterprisingly set to work herself with two helpers to create a theatre. Brambles and furze,
coarse grass and bracken were cleared, and tiers of seats constructed. Where possible the granite rocks were adapted as part of
the setting, and a permanent set was eventually built. Presenting
plays at the Minack confronts directors and actors with a variety
of problems, but being involved in a production here is a thrilling
experience. Every summer a full season takes place against a
wonderful natural backdrop of the sea and the great stone headland across the bay. This is a superb setting on a summer afternoon, and as the twilight fades at an evening performance the

effect of moonlight across the murmuring sea is magical.

Beyond the narrow inlet of Porthgwarra with its slipway for hauling boats clear of the sea we round the south-western point of the peninsula, Gwennap Head, and follow the coast to Land's End. These are majestic cliffs, the granite towering from the sea in great columns, carved by wind and water into fantastic shapes. The sequence of headlands marches on—Tol-Pedn-Penwith, Carn Lês Boel, Pordenack Point and finally the crags of Land's End. Here the coasts and the seas meet and the waves surge restlessly over the reefs where the Longships light mounts guard, while away to the south-west the Isles of Scilly lie like clouds on the horizon.

Land's End has always caught the imagination. It inspired Humphry Davy to write

On the sea
The sunbeams tremble, and the purple light
Illumes the dark Bolerium, seat of storms.
High are his granite rocks, his frowning brow
Hangs o'er the smiling ocean.

Now the visitors throng daily over the cliff-top to try to capture the spirit of Pedn-an-Laaz, 'the end of the earth'.

The spirit is best captured not on a calm day when the sea murmurs gently around the rocks but on a wild day of winter storms. Then the ocean surges in angry surf-flecked mountains and thunders with terrifying power against the cliffs; the lighthouse is shrouded in the whirl of spray which the wind batters in one's face, and one ceases to doubt the legend of Lyonnesse. Between the granite uplands of Penwith and Scilly lay a plain, fertile and populous, until the fateful day when the sea broke in, drowning the land with its woods and churches; one man alone on horseback escaped from the rushing waters to the mainland to tell the tale. So the legend runs, and there may be more in it than fancy.

For Thomas Hardy, Lyonnesse meant Cornwall, which for him had special significance. His poem speaks to all who have experienced the peculiar fascination of this western land, its unique landscape and its mystery.

When I set out for Lyonnesse,
A hundred miles away,
The rime was on the spray,
And starlight lit my lonesomeness

When I came back from Lyonnesse
A hundred miles away.

When I came back from Lyonnesse
With magic in my eyes,
All marked with mute surmise
My radiance rare and fathomless,
When I came back from Lyonnesse
With magic in my eyes!

A Guide to Cornish Place-Names

As the Celtic inhabitants of Britain retreated westwards, yielding to the pressure of successive waves of invations from the Continent, so their language became confined to the western extremities, Wales and Cornwall, which accounts for the similarity of the Welsh and Cornish languages. In Cornwall this linguistic heritage is chiefly apparent in the place-names, which make a fascinating study. Basically the majority of names consist of a noun followed by an adjective; e.g. *bal* (mine) *dhu* (black) gives us *Baldhu*, the black mine. But not all names are so straightforward, owing to such problems as initial mutation changing the beginning of the adjectives, and other elements being introduced.

Those who wish to follow the study seriously must consult one of the comprehensive guides which explore the subject in detail. However, this list of some common words which recur in Cornish names will serve as an introduction to the subject—and perhaps encourage the reader to pursue it in greater detail.

als	cliff	hayl, hayle	estuary
an	the	hen	old
bal	mine	kelly	grove
bean, vean	small	lan	sacred enclosure, church site
bod, bos	dwelling		
bounder, vounder	lane	lis, les	court, stronghold
brea	hill	lyn	pool
caer, car, gear	fort, camp	marghas	market
cam	crooked	melyn, vellan	mill
carn	rock-pile	maen, men	stone
carrek	rock	meneth	hill
chy, ty	house	meon, veor	great
cos, coose	wood	nans, nance, nant	valley
crows	cross	noweth	new
cruk	mound	parc, park	field
dinas, dinnis	castle	pen	end, head
dour	water	pol	pool, creek, arm of estuary
du, dhu, thew	black		
eglos	church	pons, pont	bridge
ennis, enys	island	porth	cove, harbour
fenten, venton	spring	res	ford
glas, las	grey, green, blue	ros, rose	heath
gollas, wollas	lower	stennack	tin-bearing ground
goon, noon, woon	down, moor	towan	sand-dune
gwartha, wartha	higher, upper	tre, tref	farm, hamlet, town, settlement
gwin, win	white		
gweal	field	treth, treath	sand, beach
gy	water, river	wheal	mine
hal, hale	moor, marsh	zawn	chasm

Sites to Visit

This list makes no pretence to being exhaustive, but is a representative selection of the best examples of the various categories. It is to be hoped that the list will complement the text in directing attention to the most interesting aspects of the county.

Henges	Castilly, Stripple Stones
Quoits	Chun, Lanyon, Mulfra, Trethevy, Zennor
Circles	Boscawen-Un, Hurlers, Merry Maidens, Nine Maidens
Hill-top sites	Carn Brea, Castle-an-Dinas, Castle Dore, Chun Castle, St Dennis, Trencrom, Warbstow Bury
Cliff castles	Black Head, Gurnard's Head, Kelsey Head, Maen Castle, The Rumps, Treryn Dinas, Trevelgue Head, Willapark
Fogous	Carn Euny, Halligye, Trewardreva
Ancient villages	Carn Euny, Chysauster
Roman milestones	Breage, St Hilary, Tintagel
Inscribed stones	King Doniert's Stone, Men Scryfa, St Hilary, Tristan Stone (Ogham writing) Lewannick, St Clement, St Kew
Crosses	Cardinham, Lanivet, Mylor, St Erth, St Mawgan, Sancreed
Wells	Callington, Madron, St Cleer, St Clether, St Neot
Rounds	Perranporth, St Just
Castles	Launceston, Restormel, Tintagel, Trematon, Pendennis, St Mawes
Bridges	Saltash, New Bridge, Horsebridge (Tamar), Newbridge, Clapper Bridge (Lynher), Treverbyn, Pantersbridge, Respryn, Lostwithiel (Fowey), Bradford, Helland, Wadebridge (Camel)
Medieval architecture	Cotehele, Golden, Poundstock, Tintagel Old Post Office, Trecarrel
Civil War sites	Lostwithiel, Restormel, Braddock, Castle Dore, Stratton, Tresillian Bridge, Pendennis
Georgian town houses	Launceston, Liskeard, Penzance, Truro
Town halls and guildhalls	Truro, St Austell, Penzance
Country houses	Antony, Boconnoc, Caerhays, Godolphin, Lanhydrock, Pencarrow, Port Eliot, Prideaux, Tregothnan, Trelissick, Trelowarren, Trerice, Trewithen
Parks and woodlands	Antony, Boconnoc, Pencarrow, Tregothnan
Almhouses	St Germans, Tregony

Methodism	Baldhu, Camborne, Charlestown, Gwennap Pit, Roseworthy, Trewint
Quakerism	Come-to-Good, Redruth, St Austell, Truro

Industrial Sites

Ports and harbours	Polperro, Fowey, Par, Charlestown, Mevagissey, Falmouth, Gweek, Newlyn, Mousehole, St Ives, Padstow, Portreath
Lighthouses	Lizard, Trevose
Canal	Bude Canal
Water mills	Morden Mill, Cotehele; St Keyne Mill
Railways	Bridges:Saltash, Calstock, St Pinnock, Truro, Treffry Viaduct Disused lines: Launceston—Wadebridge, Chacewater—Newquay; Gwinear Road—Helston Mineral lines, e.g. Devoran
Granite quarries	Cheesewring, De Lank, Lamorna, Mabe
Slate quarry	Delabole
China clay	Hensbarrow Downs, Tregonning Hill; Wheal Martyn museum, Carthew
Mining	East Pool Engines, Tolgus Tin; evidences in Camborne-Redruth area; abandoned engine-houses, e.g. Wheal Coates, Botallack
Foundries	Charlestown, Hayle, Perranarworthal

Churches

Celtic	St Piran's Oratory
Norman work	Cury, Kilkhampton, Morwenstow, St Germans, Tintagel
Georgian	Helston, St Euny Redruth, Penzance
Victorian	Truro Cathedral
Ornamented exteriors	Launceston, St Neot, Truro St Mary
Towers	Fowey, Linkinhorne, Probus, St Austell, St Buryan
Fonts	Altarnun, Bodmin, Launceston St Thomas, Lostwithiel, Morwenstow, Roche, St Austell, St Stephen-in-Brannel
Medieval tiles	Launcells
Frescoes	Breage, Poughill, Poundstock
Glass	St Kew, St Neot, St Winnow; Cardinham, Ladock, Truro Cathedral
Rood screens	Blisland, Lanreath, St Buryan, St Ewe, St Winnow
Brasses	Antony, Blisland, Cardinham, Constantine, Menheniot, Quethiock, St Mawgan
Bench-ends	Altarnun, Cardinham, Gorran, Launcells, Mullion, Poughill, St Winnow
Slate monuments	Blisland, Bodmin, Duloe, Pelynt, Talland, St Breock, St Tudy
Monuments	Bodmin, Callington, Landulph, Launceston, North Hill, Probus, St Germans, St Michael Penkevil

Index

Altarnun 44–45
Antony 29–30
Arundell family 29, 35, 64, 101, 104

Baldhu 121, 128, 140, 143
Bissoe 129, 140
Black Head 11, 71, 74, 109
Blisland 80, 97
Boconnoc 61, 62
Bodinnick 64–65
Bodmin 13, 45, 54, 78–79, 99, 118
Bodmin Moor 10, 12, 14, 16, 26, 34, 42, 45–48, 49, 52, 54, 78, 80, 110, 125, 126, 141
Boscastle 38, 39
Boscawen-Un 164
Botallack 12, 166
Braddock 61–62
Brasses 29, 35, 54, 65, 101, 123, 145, 173
Breage 152
Brown Willy 14, 46, 49, 141
Bude 35–36, 37, 38

Cadgwith 148
Caerhays 110–111, 129
Callington 20, 21, 26–27
Calstock 20–21
Camborne 13, 125, 128, 130–133, 155
Camel, River 7, 10, 43, 65, 78, 79–80, 97–100, 102, 105, 135
Camelford 36, 42, 46, 80
Canals 12, 35–36, 55, 57, 135, 173
Cape Cornwall 12, 167
Caradon Hill 27, 51, 55
Carclew 121–122, 129
Carew, Richard 29, 30, 56, 123, 164
Carn Brea 10, 15, 126, 128, 130, 136, 137, 140
Carn Euny 11, 165
Carn Marth 130, 140–141
Carnmenellis 10, 133, 139, 141, 151
Carrick Roads 14, 113, 114, 121
Castle-an-Dinas 14, 42, 80, 102
Castle Dore 63, 67
Cawsand 31, 155
Charlestown 71, 74

Cheesewring 10, 51, 55
China Clay 14, 46, 47, 70–77, 79, 115, 141
Chun Castle and Quoit 164, 165
Chysauster 11, 165–166
Civil War 20, 29, 62–64, 69, 104, 123, 146, 152, 156, 172
Clapper bridges 26, 80
Clowance 139, 156
Cober, River 150, 151
Come-to-Good 121
Constantine 145
Cornish language 7, 13, 23, 34–35, 107, 122, 147, 160, 164–165, 171
Cotehele 20, 21–22, 111
Coverack 147–148, 155
Crackington Haven 38
Cremyll 24, 29, 31, 55
Cromlechs 15, 51, 163–164, 165, 172
Crosses 11, 53, 54, 65, 106, 122, 167, 172
Cury 149–150, 155

Davy, Sir Humphry 160, 169
Delabole 43, 79, 97
De Lank River 26, 80
Devonport 24, 30, 114, 155
Devoran 121, 127, 129, 140
Dodman Point 11, 110, 141
Dozmary Pool 42, 47–48, 53
Duchy of Cornwall 20, 65, 68, 145, 168
Dupath Well 26–27

Exeter, Diocese of 15, 28, 119, 122, 141, 145

Fal, River 7, 14, 102, 110, 111–116, 121–124, 127, 139, 155
Falmouth 14, 114, 117, 122–124, 142, 155
Ferries 12, 24, 25, 29, 31, 55, 64, 98, 115, 116, 145
Fishing 13, 57–59, 109, 114, 145, 160–162
Fogous 11, 145–146, 165, 166, 172
Fonts 11, 17, 25, 44, 68, 76, 78, 100, 173
Forrabury 38–39
Fowey 63, 64–66, 68, 71, 75, 107
Fowey, River 7, 10, 11, 49–50, 52–54, 64–67, 78

Gannel 105
Germoe 73, 152
Gerrans 112, 113
Giant's Hedge 61–64
Glasney College 122
Glendurgan 145
Glynn Valley 50, 56, 79
Godolphin family 150, 152–153
Godrevy 137, 138
Golden 101, 112
Golant 66, 67
Goonhilly Down 148, 160
Gorran 110
Goss Moor 14, 102, 115
Grampound 111, 115
Granite 10, 12, 46, 51, 70, 73, 79–80, 122, 139, 166–169
Grenville family 34, 35, 62–63
Greyston Bridge 19, 20
Gribbin Head 71, 109
Gulval 11, 159, 165
Gunnislake 20, 21, 26, 55
Gunwalloe 106, 149, 155
Gurnard's Head 165, 166
Gweek 146, 150
Gwennap 139–140
Gwennap Pit 141, 142, 143
Gwithian 137, 138

Hardy, Thomas 39, 41, 169–170
Hayle 105, 125, 128, 134–135, 137
Hayle, River 10, 129, 134–135, 138, 139, 152, 155 156
Helford River 7, 14, 110, 124, 144–146, 147, 150, 155
Hell's Mouth 137, 155
Helman Tor 70, 76
Helston 126, 144, 146, 147, 150–151, 153, 154
Hensbarrow Downs 10, 14, 70, 73, 76–77, 110, 125, 126
Hill-top forts 11, 15, 18, 47, 67, 76, 102, 165, 172
Horse Bridge 20, 22, 63
Hurlers 10, 51

Illogan 136–137
Ince 25–26
Inny, River 19, 43, 44

Kelsey Head 11, 105
Kensey, River 16, 18, 43
Kilkhampton 34, 35, 36
King Harry Ferry 115, 121
Kingsand 31
Kit Hill 14, 20, 21, 26, 51
Kynance Cove 149

Ladock 116
Lamorna Cove 167, 168
Lander, Richard 118–119
Land's End 10, 134, 142, 159, 165, 167, 169
Landulph 23–24
Lanhydrock 48, 62, 69–70
Lanlivery 70
Lanreath 61
Lanteglos by Fowey 64–65
Launcells 36–37
Launceston 11, 13, 16–18, 36, 43, 45, 118

Lelant 135, 162, 163
Lighthouses 14, 37, 100, 109, 113, 148, 153, 166, 168, 169, 173
Linkinhorne 50, 51, 52
Liskeard 28, 54–55, 62, 126
Lizard 14, 15, 31, 113, 124, 144, 148–149, 153, 155
Loe Bar 150, 151, 154
Looe 29, 55, 56–57, 61
Lostwithiel 11, 49, 65, 67–69, 70, 75, 126
Ludgvan 158–159, 165
Luxulyan 70, 71, 74, 142
Lynher, River 11, 26–27, 29, 30, 46, 50, 51

Madron 159, 160
Maker 31, 32
Marazion 151, 157
Marsland Mouth 7, 32
Mawgan in Pydar 101
Mawnan 144, 146
Men-an-Tol 164, 165
Meneage 146–148
Methodism 45, 134, 141–143, 166, 167, 173
Mevagissey 109, 110
Mining 12, 20–21, 72–75, 103–104, 125–143, 151–152, 160, 166–167
Monasticism 16, 17, 28, 41, 66, 71, 78–79, 99, 113, 156
Morwenstow 32–34, 37
Mount's Bay 10, 106, 134, 144, 148–149, 153–160
Mousehole 160, 161, 167
Mullion 149
Mylor 121–122

National Trust 21, 30, 33, 38, 40, 46, 58, 64, 69, 71, 98, 100, 104, 110, 113, 121, 130, 136, 137, 144, 145, 149, 151, 156, 160, 164, 165, 166, 168
Newbridge (River Lynher) 26
New Bridge (River Tamar) 20, 26, 55
Newlyn 160, 161, 162
Newlyn East 103, 104, 105
Newquay 13, 70, 74, 75, 100, 103, 129
Norman architecture 11, 17, 25, 28, 33, 34, 41, 122, 149, 173

Opie, John 107–108
Ottery, River 18

Padstow 32, 66, 97, 98, 99–100, 107, 155
Par 71, 74, 75
Pendeen 128, 167
Pendeen Watch 166, 167
Pendennis Castle 14, 64, 104, 113, 114, 123, 124, 144
Penpoll Creek 64, 66
Penryn 122, 123, 146
Pentewan 74
Pentire Point 98
Penwith 10, 11, 15, 126, 129, 134, 158–170
Penzance 13, 128, 138, 155, 159–160, 161, 163
Percuil River 113, 114
Perranarworthal 121
Perranporth 105–106, 107, 129, 135, 136
Plymouth 20, 24, 62, 155
Plymouth Sound 21, 29, 31, 32, 161
Polperro 58–59, 155
Polruan 64
Polston Bridge 19, 20

Pont Pill 64–65
Port Eliot 27–28
Porthleven 151, 153
Porth Navas 145
Port Isaac 98
Portloe 112
Portreath 127, 128, 129, 137, 140
Portscatho 113
Poughill 35, 36, 37
Poundstock 37
Praa Sands 152, 153
Prideaux Place 99–100
Probus 51, 72, 111–112

Railways 13, 20–21, 24–25, 36, 55, 72, 74–75, 78, 123, 127, 132, 159, 162–163
Rame Head 29, 31
Rashleigh, Charles 72, 73–74
Red River 133, 134, 137, 138
Redruth 10, 13, 45, 107, 125, 127, 128, 129–130, 140, 141
Reservoirs 46, 52, 80, 139, 141, 167
Respryn Bridge 69
Restormel Castle 11, 67–69, 114
Robartes family 48, 62, 63, 69
Roche 48, 74, 76
Rocky Valley 39–40
Rood screens 18, 33, 37, 41, 44, 61, 64, 97, 99, 101, 103, 105, 111, 122, 149, 167, 173
Roughtor 46, 47, 141
Rounds 106–107, 167
Royal Albert Bridge 24–25
Ruan Lanihorne 115
Rumps Point 43, 98

St Agnes 15, 128, 135, 136, 137
St Anthony in Meneage 146–147
St Anthony in Roseland 14, 112, 113
St Austell 10, 13, 67, 70, 71–72, 73, 74, 75, 76, 141
St Breock 48, 97
St Breward 97
St Buryan 164, 167–168
St Cleer 50, 51, 52
St Columb Major 97, 101–102
St Day 140, 141
St Dennis 14, 74, 76
St Enodoc 98
St Erth 134, 138, 139, 160, 162
St Ewe 110, 111
St Germans 28, 119
St Hilary 155-156
St Ives 13, 43, 134, 141, 142, 155, 161, 162–163
St Juliot 38, 39
St Just in Penwith 102, 106, 166, 167
St Just in Roseland 106, 112, 114, 122
St Keverne 102, 144, 147, 148
St Kew 79, 97
St Mawes 114, 123
St Michael's Mount 16, 64, 125, 139, 140, 156–157, 158
St Neot 47, 49, 50, 52–54
St Piran's Oratory 106, 138
St Piran's Round 106–107
St Stephens in Brannel 73, 76
St Stephens by Launceston 16
St Stephens by Saltash 25
St Winnow 64, 106

Saints 11, 13–14, 43, 99, 106, 107, 134–135, 151
Saltash 13, 24–25, 26, 27, 55, 62, 63
Sancreed 52, 158, 165, 167
Scilly, Isles of 46, 63, 64, 152, 159, 169
Slate 12, 43, 46, 47, 55, 57, 102, 167, 173
Stained glass 21, 28, 35, 53, 64, 97, 103, 116, 120, 173
Standing stones 15, 67, 164–165
Stithians 52, 139, 141
Stratton 35, 36, 62
Stripple Stones 46–47

Talland 57
Tamar, River 7, 14, 16, 18, 19–21, 22–25, 30, 32, 36, 62, 63
Tiddy, River 27, 28
Tintagel 11, 40–42, 43
Tonacombe Manor 34
Torpoint 24, 29, 30
Towednack 166
Trade routes 10, 65, 78, 134, 156, 158
Trebarwith Strand 43
Trebetherick 99
Trecarrel 17, 19–20, 65
Treffry viaduct 71, 74–75
Tregony 101, 112, 115
Tregothnan 14, 115–116
Trelawny family 59–60
Trelissick 121
Trelowarren 146
Trematon 11, 25, 26, 28
Trencrom 15, 134, 165
Trengrouse, Henry 154
Trerice Manor 35, 104–105
Treryn Dinas 165, 169
Trethevy Quoit 51, 163
Trevaunance Cove 136, 137
Treverbyn Bridge 49
Trevisa, John of 23
Trevithick, Richard 37, 126, 131–133, 137, 138–139
Trevose Head 100, 136, 141
Trewardreva 145
Trewithen 74, 112
Truro 13, 14, 60, 69, 116–120, 123, 126, 127, 137
Truro Cathedral 11, 14, 19, 117, 119–120, 148, 149, 162
Twelveheads 140, 143
Tywardreath 71

Valency, River 38, 39
Veryan 112
Viaducts 13, 20, 24, 56, 71, 74–75, 117, 130

Wadebridge 36, 57, 78, 79, 97
Warbstow Bury 18, 42
Warleggan 50, 54
Wells, holy 26–27, 36, 43–44, 52, 53, 56, 66, 72, 78, 160, 168, 172
Wendron 146, 151
Wesley, John and Charles 15, 45, 141–143, 162, 166
Whitesand Bay 29, 31
Williams family 111, 129
Withey Brook 50
Wrestling 102, 167

Zennor 163, 165, 166
Zone Point 14, 113